POCKET **ROUGH GUIDE**

NAPLES
& THE AMALFI COAST

WALKS & TOURS

YOUR TAILOR-MADE TRIP
STARTS HERE

Tailor-made trips and unique adventures crafted by local experts

Rough Guides has been inspiring travellers with lively and thought-provoking guidebooks for more than 35 years. Now we're linking you up with selected local experts to craft your dream trip. They will put together your perfect itinerary and book it at local rates.

Don't follow the crowd – find your own path.

HOW ROUGHGUIDES.COM/TRIPS WORKS

STEP 1

Pick your dream destination, tell us what you want and submit an enquiry.

STEP 2

Fill in a short form to tell your local expert about your dream trip and preferences.

STEP 3

Our local expert will craft your tailor-made itinerary. You'll be able to tweak and refine it until you're completely satisfied.

STEP 4

Book online with ease, pack your bags and enjoy the trip! Our local expert will be on hand 24/7 while you're on the road.

BENEFITS OF PLANNING AND BOOKING AT ROUGHGUIDES.COM/TRIPS

PLAN YOUR ADVENTURE WITH LOCAL EXPERTS

Rough Guides' English-speaking local experts are hand-picked, based on their experience in the travel industry and their impeccable standards of customer service.

SAVE TIME AND GET ACCESS TO LOCAL KNOWLEDGE

When a local expert plans your trip, you save time and money when you book, even during high season. You won't be charged for using a credit card either.

MAKE TRAVEL A BREEZE: BOOK WITH PEACE OF MIND

Enjoy stress-free travel when you use Rough Guides' secure online booking platform. All bookings come with a money-back guarantee.

WHAT DO OTHER TRAVELLERS THINK ABOUT ROUGH GUIDES TRIPS?

Trip to Spain

This Spain tour company did a fantastic job to make our dream trip perfect. We gave them our travel budget, told them where we would like to go, and they did all of the planning. Our drivers and tour guides were always on time and very knowledgable. The hotel accommodations were better than we would have found on our own. Only one time did we end up in a location that we had not intended to be in. We called the 24 hour phone number, and they immediately fixed the situation.

Don A, USA ★★★★★

Trip to Morocco

Our trip was fantastic! Transportation, accommodations, guides – all were well chosen! The hotels were well situated, well appointed and had helpful, friendly staff. All of the guides we had were very knowledgeable, patient, and flexible with our varied interests in the different sites. We particularly enjoyed the side trip to Tangier! Well done! The itinerary you arranged for us allowed maximum coverage of the country with time in each city for seeing the important places.

Sharon, USA ★★★★★

PLAN AND BOOK YOUR TRIP AT ROUGHGUIDES.COM/TRIPS

CONTENTS

Introduction

Best itineraries

Directory

Ancient Wonders
Route 6 visits the archaeological sites of Pompeii and Herculaneum, while a trip to the Campi Flegrei (route 5) takes in sights from a Roman amphitheatre to the mysterious cave of the Cumaean sibyl.

Best Walks & Tours for...

Art Buffs
Naples' central churches (route 1) are full of Baroque masterpieces, and the modern art museum is an essential stop. Don't miss the Museo di Capodimonte (route 4), one of Italy's finest art museums.

Escaping the Crowds
Despite its astonishing sights, the Campi Flegrei area (route 5) is low on tourists; Capri (route 10) is heaving during the day, but at night is free of crowds; and Procida (route 12) is a sleepy refuge from the bay's busier sights.

Families
In Naples, the kid-friendly combination of castle, park and aquarium make route 3 ideal, while the friendly atmosphere of Sorrento (route 7) and the lovely beaches of Ischia (route 11) make these a good bet for families.

Foodies

For genuine Neapolitan pizza, the rowdy *centro storico* (route 1) is the place, and a fish feast in Borgo Marinaro (route 2) is a must. The Sorrentine Peninsula (route 7) has a clutch of gourmet restaurants.

Back to Nature

The Sorrentine Peninsula (route 7) is a walker's paradise, while Ischia (route 11) offers natural hot springs, and Capri (route 10) has wonderful walks. For an encounter with Mother Nature, visit Vesuvius (route 6).

Seaside Fun

Positano's beaches (route 8) are large, with plenty of facilities; the Sorrentine Peninsula (route 7) has good, tucked-away swimming spots, while Ischia and Procida (routes 11 and 12) boast lovely beaches and crystal-clear water.

Street Life

For a dose of the street life that defines the city, a stroll through Naples' *centro storico* (route 1) can't be beaten. Sorrento (route 7) and Capri (route 10) are also always bustling, too, if more genteel.

INTRODUCTION

An introduction to Naples and what makes it special, what not to miss and what to do when you're there.

Discover Naples

Disorderly, rowdy, exhilarating – the capital of the Italian South is like nowhere else. The Bay of Naples holds its own charms, from dazzling islands to slumbering volcanoes, world-class archaeological sites and the sinuous Amalfi Coast.

Naples lives by its own rules. Utterly lacking in tourist-ready gloss, the city demands that visitors give in to the flow of local life; the noise and chaos may be somewhat alarming at first, but a wander through the *centro storico* will quickly win you over.

All of human life is played out here: boys dodge the traffic to play street football; old men cluster on street corners, heatedly debating politics; mopeds bearing entire families buzz down the narrow streets, klaxons blaring and workers cram into tiny bars, putting the world to rights on their coffee break.

And those clichéd images of a bygone Italy that have all but disappeared elsewhere in the country – glittering shrines, lines of washing hung between houses across narrow streets to dry and raucous local markets – are everywhere you turn in Naples.

It is the third-largest city in Italy after Rome and Milan, with around 978,000 inhabitants. When its crowded and ever-expanding suburbs are included in the count however, the figure is 4.5 times this.

At the heart of it all, and visible for miles around, stands Vesuvius,

a potent symbol of the beauty and cruelty of nature and a huge influence on the Neapolitan character.

Beyond Naples' sprawling suburbs, nature takes over. Seek refuge from the clamorous city along the Amalfi Coast, in the rugged Sorrentine Peninsula and on the islands. There's something for everyone here, whether you're looking for a family break, a romantic getaway or a few days of solo pampering.

Geography and layout

The Bay of Naples and Amalfi Coast are part of Campania, one of the four provinces that make up southern Italy. The landscape is volcanic, its topography formed by ancient craters and the deposits left by thousands of years of volcanic activity.

The most prominent landmark on the bay is Vesuvius (1,017m/3,336ft), dormant since its last eruption in 1944. The only active crater in the region today is the Solfatara, which, according to scientists' latest warnings, is approaching a 'critical state' that could cause a large eruption.

The southern end of the bay is hemmed in by the Monti

A proud nation

Lattari, a hill range that forms the backbone of the Amalfi Coast.

Naples

Once you get your bearings, Naples is an easy city to navigate, and the main areas of interest to tourists can all be covered on foot. Driving is not a viable option – traffic is solid in the city centre, parking nightmarish and Neapolitan drivers anarchic, to say the least. To travel between city districts, stick to the cheap and easy public-transport system. Buses can be slow, and the metro is undergoing a major overhaul, but the funiculars that ferry people up and down the Vomero hill are ultra-efficient, and the trains and boats in and out of the city are plentiful and smooth running.

Day trips from Naples

Naples is a good base for exploring the historic sites in the bay area: trains to the Campi Flegrei, Pompeii and Herculaneum run frequently from the train station at Piazza Garibaldi. Try to arrive as early as you can at these busy sites, especially during the summer months, when they can be very crowded.

The bay area as far as Castellammare di Stabia is built-up, with ugly industrial estates and housing blocks at various stages of disrepair, but between the grim buildings sprout citrus trees and olive groves, and the sea and mountainous backdrop are constantly magnificent. South

Superstitious Naples

Naples seems to have spent its entire history waiting for Vesuvius to erupt, which goes some way towards explaining the local character traits of seize-the-day exuberance and a deep-seated reliance on superstitions to ward off harm. The superstitions that are part of everyday life are fascinating to outsiders: three times a year, the city holds its breath to see whether the Miracle of San Gennaro will keep its citizens safe; the elaborate shrines dotted throughout the city are eloquent and touching testimonies to the faith of the populace; La Smorfia – an archaic dream dictionary – is widely used by locals to interpret their dreams and divine the winning lottery numbers; and the *corno* – a horn-shaped lucky charm supposed to ward off the evil eye – is possibly Naples' most popular souvenir.

of Castellammare, the urban sprawl dwindles away, replaced by a captivating landscape of green hills, plunging cliffs and picture-postcard towns.

Beyond Naples

After a few days exploring the city, you will be craving some calm. The laid-back town of Sorrento is perfectly positioned for exploring the islands, the Amalfi Coast and Pompeii. If you don't want to hire a car and tackle the

The Galleria Umberto I   Outside Caffè Gambrinus

Amalfi drive yourself, the blue SITA buses run regular services between Sorrento, Positano and Amalfi.

In summer, ferries carry day-trippers from Sorrento and Naples to the islands. But to properly absorb the wild beauty of Capri's coastline and find time to relax in Ischia's hot springs after sightseeing, consider an overnight stay. Procida is so small that you could easily walk round it in a day, though it is still a pretty, peaceful place to spend the night, and only a short hop from Naples.

History

For nearly three thousand years, Naples was fought over and occupied by a succession of foreign powers. Greeks, Romans, Normans, Arabs, Angevins, Spanish and Bourbons – all left their mark, not just on the streets and buildings, but on the language, culture and character of the Neapolitans themselves. Gregarious by nature, their clan-based communities and innate disrespect for authority are rooted in centuries of foreign domination.

Art and architecture

Naples' chequered history has resulted in a variety of architectural styles, though medieval, Renaissance and Baroque churches, castles and *palazzi* predominate. Much of the art you are likely to see in Naples is in the Baroque style. This was sparked by Caravaggio, who pitched up here in 1606 after the Roman authorities put a price on his head for killing his opponent in a tennis match. A wanted man, he didn't stick around for long, but long enough to paint some of his greatest paintings and influence a new generation of artists with the revolutionary realism of his paintings. The works of his followers decorate churches and *palazzi* throughout the city.

Post-war Naples

For an insight into how Naples' recent history has shaped the city, read Norman Lewis's fascinating *Naples '44*, a no-holds memoir of the Allied occupation during World War II, when the city was stripped to its bare bones. The day-to-day dealings of the people are told as a series of humorous, tragic and astonishing anecdotes that help to shed light on some of the more eccentric characteristics of its present-day citizens.

Climate

Spring and autumn are by far the best seasons for visiting the Bay of Naples. The weather from April to June and September to October is not too hot for sightseeing but still warm enough to swim. July and August can be unpleasantly hot and humid, especially in the city (hence the August exodus, when most shops and restaurants close). These two months are also peak season, when the islands and coastal resorts swarm with tourists. Winters are generally mild, though unless the ghostly, abandoned atmosphere of resorts off-season appeals, the

The stunning semi-circular Piazza Plebiscito

Don't leave Naples without...

Trying the local tipple. *Limoncello* – the sticky, sweet local liqueur – is everywhere you look in these parts (and especially in Sorrento, see page 62). Most restaurants will serve you a shot of it at the end of your meal, or you can taste it in one of the dedicated shops in town. Sorrento's Limonoro (Via San Cesareo 49–53; tel: 081-878 5348) also sells *limoncello* sweets and chocolates; even the local *scialatielli* pasta is lemon-scented.

Listening out for Neapolitan music. Wander down any central backstreet and you're almost bound to hear Musica Napoletana being warbled through an open window. The *canzone napoletana* became a formally recognised genre in the 1830s, thanks to the Festival of Piedigrotta, a local songwriting competition. It petered out in the 1950s, but classics such as *Funiculì, Funiculà* and *O Sole Mio* remain as popular as ever. See page 22.

Grabbing a gelato. If you are in need of a cool down, pick up an ice cream at Gay Odin (see page 36), Chalet Ciro (see page 45) or Fantasia Gelati (points across the city, including Via Toledo 381; www.fantasiagelati.it),

some of the city's best gelaterie. If you really want to fit in, do as the locals do and have one during the customary evening *passeggiata*, or promenade.

Eating a pizza. The city is the birthplace of pizza, with the authentic Neapolitan variety having a thin crust and being cooked quickly in a wood-fired oven. Di Matteo (see page 36) is a good place to try it.

Spire-spotting. Keep an eye out for the soaring guglie (marble spires) that embellish three of the old town's squares visited on route 1, see page 30. The first, dedicated to the Virgin, stands outside the Gesù Nuovo church; the second, on Piazza San Domenico, gave thanks for the end of the plague epidemic; the third, in Piazza Sisto Riario Sforza, was erected in honour of San Gennaro, Naples' patron saint, when the city escaped unscathed after Vesuvius erupted in 1631.

Eating for free. Partake of the fine Italian tradition of the *aperitivo*. Head into a wine bar around 6pm and you'll probably find an array of bar snacks laid out for free. In some places, you can eat so much that you may not have room for dinner. See page 19.

coastal areas are less inviting. Bathing facilities close in early October and many restaurants and hotels close between November and Easter.

People and customs

Like the rest of the Italian south, the pace here is unhurried, and the easy-going locals place importance on the simple things in life – mainly good food and good company. As a generalisation, Neapolitans (like all Italians) seem to be united in their belief in the importance of the family. This can be seen in the ritual of large communal Sunday lunches, elderly parents living with their married offspring and the reluctance of young people to leave home until they get married. Although financial concerns, especially high rents, contribute to this, so does *mammismo*, the cult of the mother, whereby many young men rely on a doting mother to do their washing and cooking. However, as more Italian women develop careers, this may be the last generation of this.

Religion

Italy is a Roman Catholic society, but a tolerant one. Despite an authoritarian pope, abortion and divorce are legal and contraception is widely accepted. Indeed, much to the chagrin of the Vatican, Italy has the lowest birth rate in Europe. According to a recent survey, around 85 per cent of Italians claim to be Catholics, but only a quarter attend Mass regularly. Nonetheless, Catholicism still plays an important role in rituals, from first Holy Communion to the marriage ceremony and burials and it has an overall stronger hold in the south.

Tourism

Compared with other major Italian cities, Naples stubbornly refuses to make many concessions to tourism, so patience is essential: just trying to get across town can be something of an odyssey, thanks to its permanently clogged streets. The post-lunch siesta is commonly observed, and much of Naples shuts down on Sundays.

You won't find English spoken everywhere in Naples, though staff in hotels and shops usually speak a little. Any attempts to speak Italian are greatly appreciated.

Politics and economics

Southern Italy suffers from high unemployment, poor infrastructure and a thriving black market. Attempts to address the problems of Italy's north–south divide and to combat corruption are to little avail: the Camorra, the local branch of the mafia, is one of Italy's most powerful organised-crime networks. That said, the problem areas are on the outskirts and the tourist areas are as safe as in any other Italian city.

The biggest growth industry is tourism but beyond Naples' grim industrial suburbs, swathes of vineyards, olive groves and citrus orchards ensure a reasonable income from agriculture, too.

Politically, Naples has neither been strongly to the right nor to the left. Since World War II, both Christian Democrats and Democratic Socialists governed the city with equal frequency. However, in 2016 Luigi de Magistris, a former mafia prosecutor was re-elected mayor, running as an independent.

Beautiful artwork in a city church

Top tips for exploring Naples and the Amalfi Coast

Antiques market. During the Fiera Antiquaria Napoletana (www.fiera antiquarianapoletana.it), antiques sellers set up their wares between the Villa Comunale and Via Caracciolo on the waterfront, selling anything from old armoires to Christmas crib figurines. The market takes place on the third Sunday of the month and the preceding Saturday (except Aug), and the fourth Sunday of the month and preceding Saturday (except Jun–Aug), from 8am to 2pm.

Budget opera. If you're aged under 30, on a budget and fancy a night out at the opera, you're in luck in Naples. Discounted tickets to world-class performances at the Teatro San Carlo are available to under-30s for around €20.

Sightseeing shuttle. A shuttle bus service run by City Sightseeing (www.napoli.city-sightseeing.it) starts in Piazza Treiste e Trento and runs to the Museo di Capodimonte every hour from 9.15am to 5.15pm, taking in the Museo Archeologico en route. Tickets are €7 (see page 106).

Reaching the coast. If the Amalfi Coast is your main destination and you're on a budget, consider breaking your journey from the airport with a night in Sorrento, as there is no direct transport from the airport to the coast and the trip involves a number of buses and several hours.

Guided walks. Giovanni Visetti (tel: 339-694 2911; www.giovis.com) is an experienced walking guide with a wealth of knowledge on trails all over the coast. Giovanni also runs a walking club – experienced hikers are welcome to join the walks for free. Alternatively, check out the free guided walks at www.hikingcampania.com.

A cheap eat. Eating out in Capri can eat into your budget. Da Brioches, an excellent *alimentari* at 5 Via Fuorlovado in Capri Town (daily 8am–8.30pm), will make you up a panino for a few euros and sells plenty of tasty treats for a picnic.

Budget pampering. If your budget won't quite stretch to a spa, head to the little bay of Sorgeto, near Forio, accessible by sea or down a long flight of steps, where hot mineral springs and fumeroles bubble up under the sea, even in the depths of winter. It's also worth knowing that you can get into the Giardini Poseidon Park an hour before closing for around €5 (the day rate is €32).

Diving off Procida. The island's limpid blue waters are perfect for diving. Procida Diving Centre (tel: 081-896 8385; www.vacanzeaprocida. it) organises dives from €45, with instructor and equipment.

A yachter's paradise   Ancient Pompeii

Food and Drink

With an abundance of fresh produce, and a populace that takes its food very seriously, you may be tempted to give in to gluttony in Naples. Whether you're snacking on pizza or tucking into a seafood feast, expect to be left wanting more.

The Italians' passion for food makes them demanding customers, which means that standards are universally high: you'll eat well even in the humblest of backstreet trattorias. Queues of locals are always a good sign – if they think the food's worth waiting for, then it invariably is. On Sundays and special occasions, a family day out involves an extended, multi-course lunch. The established seafront restaurants are inundated with hungry Neapolitans at weekends, so to avoid disappointment it's best to book.

Local cuisine

The defining characteristics of the local cuisine are freshness and simplicity. Thanks to the balmy climate and fertile volcanic terrain, the raw materials are of an exceptionally high quality, which is why pizza simply topped with ripe tomatoes, basil and local olive oil seems to taste better here than it does anywhere else on the planet. Aside from pizza, most menus in this coastal area revolve around fish *(pesce)*, seafood *(frutti di mare)* and pasta.

Street food

Naples is ideal for lunch on the run: *friggitorie* sell pizza by the slice, as well as delicious fried snacks that make a great picnic lunch. Try *arancini* (breaded rice balls stuffed with minced meat or mozzarella*)*, *crocchè* (potato croquettes), *scagliuozze* (fried polenta) or *sciurilli* (fried courgette blossom). And look out for places selling a *cuoppo*, a cone of paper filled with calamari, prawns and anchovies, fried as you wait.

Pizza

Naples is the birthplace of pizza. The authentic Neapolitan variety has a thin crust and is cooked quickly in a wood-fired oven. The classics are the *marinara* (oil, tomatoes, oregano and garlic) and the *margherita* (mozzarella, tomatoes and basil), Naples' bestseller. The theory that it was named after the Queen of Savoy, wife of the first Italian king, who appreciated its patriotic red, green and white topping, is not true, though what the truth is, nobody knows. Other local favourites are the *capricciosa* (mozzarella, tomato, mushrooms, artichokes, olives and prosciutto) and

Naples is the birthplace of pizza

calzone or ripieno (folded and stuffed with mozzarella, ricotta and salami).

Pasta

Pasta with seafood *(alla pescatora)* is a menu staple: *spaghetti alle vongole* (spaghetti with clams) and *zuppa di cozze* (mussel soup) are typical *primi (first courses)*. *Spaghetti ai ricci di mare* (sea urchins) is a Procidan speciality. Non-fish dishes include *pasta e fagioli* (pasta and beans), *pasta alla puttanesca* (tomatoes, olives, capers and chilli), and ravioli with ricotta and tomato sauce, Capri's speciality. *Scialatielli* is popular in Sorrento and along the Amalfi Coast, usually served with seafood, although sometimes with cannellini beans.

Fish and seafood

Fish as a main course is simply prepared, but always fresh. Try it grilled *(alla griglia)*, fried *(fritto)* or cooked in a light broth *(all'acqua pazza)*. Squid and octopus *(polpo)* are Neapolitan favourites, usually stewed in a sauce of tomatoes, olive oil, peppers and garlic. *Fritto misto* is a popular dish of small fish from the bay, with the fish served fried, while *zuppa di pesce* (fish soup), more of a hearty stew than a soup, is eaten as a main course with toast.

Meat

Although fish is predominant, most menus offer at least a couple of meaty options. *Carne al ragù* is a

---

Food and Drink prices

Throughout this book, price ranges for a two-course meal for one with a glass of house wine are as follows:
€€€€ = Over €8
€€€ = €50–8
€€ = €25-50
€ = Under €25

---

typical dish made with rolls of meat cooked very slowly in a tomato sauce. *Coniglio all'ischitana* (rabbit stew) is an Ischian classic; Procida has its own version. *Sartù* is an elaborate ring-shaped rice dish stuffed with a variety of meat and vegetables.

Vegetables

The cornerstone of Campanian cooking is the *pomodoro* – the humble tomato. A little oil, onion, garlic, basil, parsley, maybe some capers and black olives to complement sun-ripened tomatoes, preferably the oblong San Marzano variety, known for their sweetness, go into making *salsa alla napoletana*. *Pomodorini* (cherry tomatoes) also make regular appearances in sauces and salads. *Parmigiana di melanzane*, an aubergine, tomato and mozzarella bake, is a delicious vegetarian option. Typical *contorni* (side dishes) include *scarola* and *friarelli* (local bitter greens) and *caponata*, similar to ratatouille, but with a generous dose of capers.

Delights at Caffè Gambrinus

Cheeses

Campanian mozzarella is made from buffalo milk and has a distinctively milky taste and velvety texture. It is usually eaten as a starter with basil and tomato (*insalata caprese*), and is a key pizza ingredient. Mozzarella in *carrozza* ('in a carriage') is a thick slice of mozzarella fried between two slices of bread. Cow's-milk *scamorza* is delicious when smoked (*affumicata*) and grilled. Fresh ricotta is widely used both in savoury dishes and cakes.

Ice cream

Ice cream (*gelato*) comes in a bewildering choice of flavours and is an essential accessory to the customary evening *passeggiata*, or promenade. To ensure it's the real deal, check that it's *artigianale* (home-made). *Granita*, a crushed-ice drink usually flavoured with lemon, is wonderful on a hot day.

The menu

Lunch (*pranzo*) and dinner (*cena*) traditionally involve a starter (*antipasto*), followed by a 'first course' (*primo*) of pasta, risotto or soup, and a 'second course' (*secondo*) of fish or meat accompanied by a side serving of vegetables (*contorni*), ordered separately, rounded off with dessert (*dolce*). That said, it is perfectly acceptable to share a plate of *antipasti*, then have a main course, say, or order simply a plate of pasta at lunch, if a multi-course meal seems too much.

If you're having difficulty choosing, an *antipasto misto* (an assortment of starters) is a good way to sample local specialities. A typical mixed platter might include mozzarella, prosciutto and/or salami, fish or potato croquettes, *bruschetta* and grilled vegetables. And if you're really unsure of what to order and you're happy to experiment, ask the waiter to bring you *un piatto tipico* (a local dish).

Where to eat

The variety of venues dedicated to eating and drinking – from basic pizzerias to gourmet fine-dining restaurants – is testimony to the important place that food holds in Neapolitans' hearts. It is worth remembering that price and formality aren't necessarily an indicator of quality: that unprepossessing backstreet trattoria is likely to surprise you with a meal worthy of far fancier establishments.

Snacks

You are never more than five minutes from a café, pastry shop (*pasticceria*) or ice-cream parlour (*gelateria*). Savoury snacks and cakes are usually eaten standing up or on the hoof. However, in summer there are plenty of pavement cafés with outdoor seating where you can nurse a drink, chat and people-watch for as long as you like.

Meals

Restaurant meals are eaten in either a ristorante or the traditionally

Pastiera napoletana, traditionally eaten at Easter

simpler trattoria or osteria – though the distinction is somewhat blurred these days. Many restaurants serve pizza too, but pizzerias generally offer only pizza; a pizza *al taglio* is usually a hole-in-the-wall pizzeria selling slices to take away. A *tavola calda* is a cheap self-service place, offering hot and cold dishes.

Drinks

The wines of the Italian south are enjoying a renaissance, and Campania produces some excellent varieties, benefiting from an abundance of indigenous grapes and a favourable climate. The best of the local wines, such as Fiano and Falanghina, derive from ancient varieties introduced by the Greeks and Romans, and may well be the forebears of the more renowned Cabernet and Chardonnay. Greco di Tufo is a dry white, ideal with fish dishes or soups, while Falanghina and Fiano di Avellino are fruity yet dry. Ischia produces good local whites, notably Biancolella, cultivated on the steep slopes of Monte Epomeo.

Among the reds, the *aglianico* grape reigns supreme; Italy's longest-cultivated variety, it is thought to have been introduced to Campania by the Greeks in around 750 BC. Nowadays, the grape goes into making the highly prized, full-bodied Taurasi.

Dinner is preceded by *aperitivi* – traditionally Prosecco – and followed by *digestivi* such as *grappa*,

> ## Life is sweet
> There are *pasticcerie* everywhere you look in Naples, their shelves groaning with an abundance of pastries in every form: stuffed with cream, dusted with icing sugar, topped with glazed fruit, or slathered in chocolate. Neapolitan classics include rum-soaked *babà* and *sfogliatelle*, fine-layered, shell-shaped pastry filled with orange-flavoured ricotta – as well as seasonal favourites such as *struffoli* (puffed-up balls of dough drenched in honey) at Christmas, and *zeppole di San Giuseppe* (deep-fried doughnuts stuffed with custard), baked to celebrate the saint's day on 19 March. *Pastiera napoletana*, a ricotta cheesecake scented with orange blossom, has been baked to celebrate Easter for centuries.

the Italian firewater. For those with a sweeter tooth, there is *limoncello*, a strong but sweet lemon liqueur.

The morning coffee is usually knocked back at the counter rather than lingered over (and you'll be charged around double for the privilege of sitting down). Italians everywhere like to end a meal with a *caffè*, and the Neapolitan espresso is hailed as the best in the country, served very hot and very strong; if you like it weaker, ask for a macchiato (with a drop of hot milk).

Tomatoes and mozzarella – a staple light lunch   Limoncello, a favourite tipple

Shopping

Naples and the Amalfi Coast may not compete with Rome and Milan in terms of designer shopping, but a wealth of independent boutiques, traditional crafts and lively neighbourhood markets keep diehard shoppers amused.

Naples' main attraction for shoppers lies in the individuality of its boutiques and specialist shops, and the atmosphere of its shopping streets. To shop as the locals do, punctuate your spending spree with plenty of breaks for *gelato* and coffee.

Naples

Whatever you buy, take home a local speciality to remind you of your trip: a bottle of *limoncello*, some spicy salami, a set of Christmas crib figurines or a pair of made-to-measure sandals.

Designer fashion

Most up-market designer shops are in Chiaia. Via dei Mille and Via dei Filangeri, and their side streets, are crammed with boutiques selling clothes, shoes, leather, jewellery and soft furnishings. Big-name designers – Ferragamo, Armani, Versace, Gucci, et al – cluster around Piazza dei Martiri and Via Calabritto. Finely crafted bags, belts and leather goods can be found at **Tramontano** (Via Chiaia 143) while **Marinella**'s legendary ties are worn by royalty and film stars (Riviera di Chiaia 287).

Mainstream fashion

More affordable fashions can be found on Via Toledo at chains such as Benetton and Stefanel. The street is lined with pavement hawkers selling designer imitations such as bags, etc. – haggling is expected. The Galleria Umberto I, an elegant nineteenth-century shopping arcade, is a retreat from the heat. Vomero is home to the department store **Coin** (Via Scarlatti 90–98; www.coin.it), while Chiaia has the cheaper **Upim** (17 Via Nicola Nisco; www.upim.it).

Arts and crafts

The *centro storico*, particularly along and around Spaccanapoli, is filled with artisans' workshops, jewellers, grocery stores and specialist shops. You will often find an entire street dedicated to one particular product: Via San Sebastiano has back-to-back music shops; Via Santa Maria di Costantinopoli is good for antiques. A good place for a Neapolitan souvenir is Via di San Gregorio Armeno, full of stalls selling terracotta figures and kitsch paraphernalia for the decoration of Christmas cribs *(presepi)*, alongside *smorfia* boards (a kind of dream-

Local pottery

interpreting lotto game) and horn-shaped good-luck charms – descendants of the phallic amulets of Pompeii.

Jewellery

The ancient art of engraving and cameo-making is still practised in Naples and in the factories of Torre del Greco on the outskirts. Spaccanapoli has several jewellers selling traditional designs, while the streets south of Corso Umberto and west of Via Duomo are the domain of gold- and silversmiths.

Amalfi Coast

The bright ceramics made around the Amalfi Coast, particularly Vietri sul Mare, are highly prized. Workshops *(botteghe)* are dotted along the coastal road, though it's not always easy to stop. Ravello and Amalfi have a good choice of shops selling quality ceramics. The **Amatruda family** (www.amatruda. it) operates the last of Amalfi's paper mills, producing handmade paper that is sold in beautifully packaged boxes all over town. Positano is known for its clothes, swimwear and sandals.

Sorrento

The main shopping street, Corso Italia, is dominated by fashion, footwear and jewellery stores; the more up-market boutiques are west of Piazza Tasso. The narrow pedestrian streets of Via San Cesareo and Via Fuoro are full of souvenir shops, selling lemon-themed teatowels, ceramics

Naples' markets

Naples' street markets are great hunting grounds for foodie souvenirs – and offer an authentic slice of Neapolitan life in all its chaotic, colourful glory. Towards the station, the market around Porta Nolana is famous for its fish, but also sells fruit and vegetables. Via Pignasecca, the heart of working-class Naples, climbs from Piazza Carità (at the end of the pedestrianised section of Via Toledo) to Montesanto station. It's heaven for bargain-hunters and food-lovers, with its hotchpotch of fruit, fish and tripe stalls, bakeries and delis, and a great place to pick up salamis and cheeses. The tiny food shops and stalls along Via dei Tribunali are good for *taralli* (Neapolitan savoury pastries), biscuits, pasta and wine.

and soaps, as well as leather bags, lace and the ubiquitous *limoncello*. Marquetry *(intarsio)* is Sorrento's other speciality. For quality pieces, visit **A. Gargiulo & Jannuzzi** (Viale E. Caruso 1; www.gargiulo-jannuzzi.it).

Capri

The streets between the Piazzetta, Via Vittorio Emanuele and Via Camerelle are home to the top names in fashion, with prices to match. For a cheaper souvenir, visit **Carthusia** (Viale Matteotti 2d).

Via San Gregorio Armeno

Cameos are popular in Naples

Entertainment

Performance is part of Neapolitan life. The locals' innate flair for entertainment and penchant for theatrics are reflected in the city's cultural life, from world-class opera to classical concerts under the stars.

Naples is best known for its opera, but, as seems fitting for this earthy, down-to-earth city, it's the more populist, home-grown *canzone napoletana* that you're most likely to hear during your visit. Theatre in Naples is an Italian-only realm; the main venue is the **Teatro Bellini** (www.teatrobellini.it).

Plenty of concerts and events are organised, particularly in summer, but nightlife generally revolves around eating and drinking. The best way to enjoy the balmy nights is to join the locals for a postprandial stroll, with the essential ice-cream stop along the way.

Music

Naples' Teatro San Carlo makes a grand backdrop to the world-class performances that take place there, while on the coast and islands, a concert with a view is not to be missed.

The **Teatro San Carlo** (www.teatro sancarlo.it) is the oldest working opera house in Europe and Italy's best after Milan's La Scala. The season runs from January to mid-July, and from September to December. Buy tickets in the theatre box office or from the ticket office in **Galleria Umberto I**, opposite (www.boxofficenapoli.it).

Outside Naples, classical-music lovers are well catered for all summer long. During the Sorrento Festival, concerts are held in the picturesque cloister of San Francesco church, while the prestigious Ravello Festival (www.ravellofestival.com), centred on the Villa Rufolo gardens, draws an international crowd. In Capri, open-air concerts are staged at the Certosa di San Giacomo and Villa San Michele. The neoclassical villas in and around Ercolano play host to the Festival delle Ville Vesuviane (www.villevesuviane.net).

Commedia dell'arte

The *Commedia dell'arte*, in which stock characters play out a variety of plots on the eternal themes of love, jealousy, revenge and death, has ancient roots in Naples. Look out for Pulcinella – the female equivalent of Britain's Mr Punch – who crops up on any number of souvenirs, from puppets to keyrings, across the city. Performances these days are rare.

Teatro San Carlo

Film

Virtually all English-language films are dubbed into Italian. Naples' film festival in June offers a rare opportunity to see films in their original language (www.napolifilmfestival.com).

Nightlife

The liveliest places after dark are the main piazzas of the old town, especially around the university district, where the majority of late-night bars and live-music venues are clustered. Chiaia, too, has a lively after-dark scene, with chic cocktail lounges and some trendy clubs; be sure to dress up. Listings of what's on where can be found in the local newspaper, *Il Mattino*, or drop in at the tourist office for information and free entertainment guides.

During the summer, many city venues close and beach bars turn into clubs. The best place along the coast for all-night dancing is Positano.

Festivals

Each city, town and village has its own patron saint, and their feast day *(festa)* is celebrated with parades and processions, elaborate costumes, singing and dancing, fireworks and feasting. Summer is the season for classical-music festivals, most of which begin in July. Autumn festivals, known as *sagre*, are linked to the land and harvest time.

Annual events

The first major celebration of the year is Easter week, with large-scale Good Friday processions; Procida's is one of the most dramatic. In Naples, the thrice-yearly Festa di San Gennaro, the first of which is in May, is not to be missed if you're in the city. Also in May, the Maggio dei Monumenti allows access to historic buildings normally closed to the public (ask at the tourist office for a programme).

From July to September, open-air concerts take place in the spectacular Villa Rufolo in Ravello. July is a bumper month for saints' days: on the 16th, the bell tower of the church of the Madonna del Carmine on Naples' Piazza del Mercato explodes with fireworks; on the 26th, the patron saint of Ischia, Sant'Anna, is honoured with a torchlit procession of hundreds of boats; the 27th is the Festa di San Pantaleone, with the liquefaction of the saint's blood and a fireworks display in Ravello.

August 15 is Ferragosto (the feast of the Assumption) and a national holiday. Positano has a procession to commemorate the landing of the Saracens, followed by yet more pyrotechnics. September sees the Piedigrotta Festival, a traditional celebration of Neapolitan songs, as well as Pizzafest.

Finally, Christmas *(Natale)* in Naples is a colourful affair: churches compete to build the finest *presepe* (Nativity scene), and concerts are held around the city.

Nativity scene art pieces

Activities

This famed stretch of coast offers opportunities galore for outdoor types: hire a boat, take a diving course or stick to dry land and tackle one of the hiking trails that crisscross the countryside.

Naples' open spaces are perfect for running and cycling, but for swimming and watersports you're better off heading along to the coast. Ischia is famous for its spas.

Swimming

Most of the coastline from Naples to Salerno is rocky, and beaches are not always accessible or easy to find. In the Naples area, the cleanest water is at Posillipo, located west of town, although the beaches tend to be extremely packed and overrun in high season.

On the Sorrentine Peninsula, the Bay of Ieranto is many people's idea of a perfect, hidden-away beach; Sorrento itself is less blessed, though there are plenty of *stabilimenti* (beach clubs) where you can lounge around in the sun. Some of the fancier hotels in Sorrento and Amalfi have lifts down to the sea and their own seawater pools and private beaches.

The Amalfi Coast's grey-sand beaches are not the most picturesque, but Positano's and Amalfi's are broad at least, and the sea is clear enough.

Capri's shore, although pebbly, offers lots of opportunities for a dip; Marina Grande is the most accessible, but the section by the Blue Grotto is more appealing, with platforms carved out of the rock and ladders down to the sea.

Ischia has some lovely sandy beaches; the Baia di San Montano and the Spiaggia dei Maronti are the ones to head for.

On Procida, the Lido and Chiaia are the nicest beaches.

Super-fit swimmers compete in the Gulf Marathon (www.capri napoli.com) every year in June, an epic 36km (22-mile) slog from Capri's Marina Grande to Naples' seafront.

Diving

The Gulf of Naples offers plenty of opportunities for experienced divers and beginners alike, and there are a number of dive centres offering diving trips, courses and equipment for hire. On the mainland, try Centro Sub Costiera Amalfitana at Praiano; https://centrosubcostiera amalfitana.com).

On Ischia, contact Ischia Diving Centre in Ischia Porto (www.ischiadiving.net). Procida's

Beach life in Positano

limpid blue waters are perfect for diving. Procida Diving Centre (www.vacanzeaprocida.it) organise dives with an instructor and equipment included in the fee.

Diving in the Campi Flegrei is a unique and rewarding excursion (Centro Sub Campi Flegrei; www.centrosubcampiflegrei.it), and the crystal-clear waters of the protected Marine Park of Punta della Campanella on the Sorrentine Peninsula is another popular spot (www.puntacampanelladiving.com).

Boating

You can hire boats all along the coast. In Procida, try Blue Dream (tel: 081-896 0579; www.bluedreamcharter.com), which rents yachts and runs a sailing school. If a yacht is beyond your budget, try Ippocampo (tel: 081-896 77 64; www.ippocampo.biz), which rents dinghies and the local *gozzi* boats, as well as organising diving excursions, both during the day and at night.

In Ischia, Capitan Morgan (tel: 081-985 080; www.capitanmorgan.it) runs inexpensive boat trips that take visitors round the island and to other points along the coast. In Capri, Gruppo Motoscafisti (www.motoscafisticapri.com) operates boat trips, while Capritime (www.capritime.com) offers small-group boat tours with a skipper. For more information on boat trips from Positano around the Amalfi Coast, read the 'Boat trips' box (see page 69).

Walking

The Sorrentine peninsula, the Monti Lattari and Amalfi Coast, Ischia and Capri all offer scenic walking trails, many of which have been marked out by the Club Alpino Italiano (CAI). The maps of the Sorrentine Peninsula and Ischia and Procida published by Kompass are useful tools for hikers. Footpaths have also been marked out on the slopes of Mount Vesuvius and Monte Faito. Local tourist offices supply free walking maps.

For organised excursions, Giovanni Visetti (tel: 339-694 2911) is a friendly and knowledgeable local guide; his website, www.giovis.com, is an excellent resource.

Running

The annual Naples Marathon (www.napolirunning.com) is held in mid-April and the scenic route takes in the city centre and the Lungomare. There's also a half-marathon and a 4km (2.5-mile) fun run for a less strenuous workout. If you just want a leisurely jog, the broad, sweeping Lungomare is the perfect place for it; alternatively, head for the tranquil 124-hectare Bosco di Capodimonte where you can take to the paths and enjoy the beautifully manicured gardens at your own pace.

If you can afford it, rent a boat

Exploring Pompei

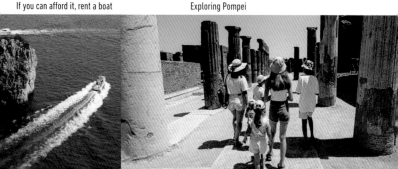

Chronology

Naples' history is woven into the city's fabric: the layout of the centro storico follows the grid of ancient Neapolis beneath it, while invaders from the French to the Spanish built churches and palazzi in distinctive architectural styles.

Greeks and Romans

c.700 BC Greeks establish a colony at Parthenope.

474 BC Greeks defeat the Etruscans and establish the new city of Neapolis near Parthenope. The two cities eventually merge to form one.

c.400 BC Neapolis is commercial capital of Campania, northernmost province of Magna Graecia.

326 BC Rome conquers Neapolis.

26 BC Tiberius retires to Capri, from where he rules the Roman Empire.

AD 79 Vesuvius erupts, destroying Pompeii and Herculaneum.

324 Constantine becomes the first Christian Roman Emperor, ruling the Empire from Constantinople.

Goths, Lombards and Normans

536 Naples falls to the Eastern Empire.

568 The Lombards start to overrun Italy, and the south is divided between Byzantine and Lombard rulers.

1139 Naples falls to the Normans.

1194 Henry VI of Germany conquers the Norman kingdom of Sicily and becomes King of Naples.

Holy Roman Emperor Frederick II (1211-1250)

1197–1250 Frederick, Henry's son, achieves absolute rule over the city, bringing good government and founding Naples' first university.

The Angevins and Aragonese

1266 Kingdom of Naples given to the French royal house of Anjou.

1268 Charles makes Naples his royal residence.

1309–43 Robert of Anjou becomes King of Naples and brings Giotto and Petrarch to the court.

A victim of the AD 79 eruption at Pompeii

1503 Naples is ruled by Spanish viceroys for the next two centuries.
1529 Plague rages in the city. Over 60,000 people perish.
1538 The Campi Flegrei supervolcano erupts and forms a new mountain.
1647 Poverty and oppression provoke a massive people's revolt led by a Neapolitan fisherman, Masaniello but violently quashed.
1656 Plague returns, claiming over 250,000 of Naples' inhabitants.

The Bourbons

1738 Austria loses power over the Kingdoms of Naples and Sicily to the Spanish Bourbons.
1806 Napoleon's brother, Joseph Bonaparte, takes control of Naples.
1815 Bourbons back on the throne after Napoleon's Waterloo defeat.
1860 Garibaldi defeats the Bourbons and enters Naples, making it part of a newly unified Kingdom of Italy.
1880–1914 More than 2.5 million Italians emigrate to the Americas.
1884 Severe cholera epidemic.

World War II to the present day

1943 Naples is bombed by Allied forces. After a four-day uprising by the people, the German occupying troops are driven from the city.
1980 Campania is struck by earthquake, with 3,000 killed.
1995 Naples is listed as a UNESCO World Heritage site
2002 The lira is replaced by the euro.

Garibaldi statue in Naples

2006 Roberto Saviano publishes Gomorrah, documenting the influence of the Camorra in every aspect of Neapolitan life. He receives death threats and has since lived under police protection.
2011 Luigi de Magistris, a former mafia prosecutor, elected the city's mayor.
2012 Allegations of blackmail, extortion and illicit contract manipulation regarding the city's waste management department arise.
2016 Luigi de Magistris is re-elected mayor.
2021 University professor and seismologist Gaetano Manfredi elected mayor.
2023 Researchers at University College London announce that the Campi Flegrei supervolcano is edging close to eruption.

Mayor Luigi De Magistris

The Bay of Naples by Auguste Renoir

BEST ITINERARIES

WALK 1
The Centro Storico

The atmospheric alleys of Naples' historic centre harbour many of the city's most intriguing sights, and give a real flavour of its exhilarating street life. Wander the ancient streets and feast your eyes: this is Naples at its heady, high-octane best.

DISTANCE: 3.5km (2.25 miles)
TIME: A full day
START: Piazza del Gesù Nuovo
END: Piazza Bellini
POINTS TO NOTE: You won't be able to visit all the churches mentioned in one day, especially as many close around noon, either for the rest of the day or until around 4pm. One option is to split the itinerary into two, allocating one morning to Spaccanapoli and another to Via dei Tribunali. If you're short of time, the most interesting are Santa Chiara, the Sansevero chapel, the Duomo and San Lorenzo Maggiore. The area is at its liveliest in the evening, so be sure to come back for dinner in one of the area's many pizzerias – a quintessential Naples experience.

Naples' *centro storico* is a dense network of shadowy, narrow alleys and small squares built on the site of ancient Neapolis. Fanning upwards from the harbour and bordered by Via Toledo to the west and Piazza Garibaldi to the east, the old town is crammed with everything from cavernous churches and grand *palazzi*, to cramped houses, shops and cafés. The most interesting sights are concentrated along two parallel east–west thoroughfares that formed part of the ancient street grid: Spaccanapoli and Via dei Tribunali.

Spaccanapoli

Spaccanapoli (literally, 'split Naples') is the series of narrow streets that run in a line from Via Toledo to the Greek walls.

Chiesa del Gesù Nuovo

The walk starts at Piazza del Gesù Nuovo, a bustling square dominated by the grey ashlar facade of the **Chiesa del Gesù Nuovo** ❶ (www.gesunuovo.it; tel: 081 557 8111; free), originally part of a Renaissance *palazzo* that was converted into a church by Jesuits in 1597. The Baroque interior is filled with fine frescoes, paintings and

Via dei Tribunali

sculptures, including works by the Spanish artist José Ribera (1590–1652) and the master of Neapolitan Baroque Luca Giordano (1632–1705).

Santa Chiara

The first of Spaccanapoli's streets is Via Benedetto Croce. Immediately on the right stands the **convent of Santa Chiara 2** (www.monastero disantachiara.it; charge). Although bomb damage during World War II destroyed much of the interior, reconstruction has preserved the austere character of the original church, built in the early fourteenth

Tiles at the convent of Santa Chiara

century for Robert of Anjou. His tomb lies behind the main altar. Fragments of a fresco by Giotto can be seen in the convent choir. The serene cloister, decorated with majolica tiles and planted with citrus trees, is – with reason – one of the most photographed corners of Naples. A small museum displays a selection of liturgical objects salvaged from the bomb wreckage, but even more interesting is the excavated area that reveals parts of an old Roman bath complex (first century AD).

A few paces further on the right is **Gay Odin**, see 1, a good excuse to stop for an ice cream.

San Domenico Maggiore

Next stop is Piazza San Domenico Maggiore, flanked by 16th- to seventeenth-century *palazzi* and the Gothic church of **San Domenico Maggiore** 3 (https://domasan domenicomaggiore.it; charge). One of several churches commissioned by Charles I of Anjou, it was given a Baroque makeover in the seventeenth century, then remodelled in the nineteenth century in an attempt to restore something of its Gothic grandeur. The upper gallery of the treasury is lined with the tombs of kings and nobles of the Aragonese court. The inlaid marble altar and balustrade is by Cosimo Fanzago (1591–1678), leading sculptor and architect of his day.

Cappella Sansevero

Take a left turn up Via Domenico Maggiore, then right on to Via Francesco de Sanctis for one of Naples' unmissable sights, the **Cappella Sansevero** 4 (www.museosansevero.it; charge). The burial chapel of the noble di Sangro family is crammed with sculptural monuments commissioned by Raimondo di Sangro, seventh prince of Sansevero (1710–71). The prince, a gifted scientist and inventor, was obsessed with alchemy – the two cadavers in the crypt are supposedly the product of one of his wild experiments. In the centre of the nave is the eerily lifelike *Cristo Velato* (Veiled Christ) by Giuseppe Sammartino, sculpted in 1753. The rendering in alabaster of the soft folds and the translucence of the veil draped over Christ's prostrate body is remarkable.

Back on the square, stop for a coffee at the historic **Scaturchio**, see 2.

Via di San Gregorio Armeno

Proceed along Spaccanapoli (you are now on Via San Biagio dei Librai), past the recently restored **statue of the Nile** 5 on your left. The reclining figure is the Egyptian river god; the cherubs symbolise the river's tributaries. Peek into the tiny Bar Nilo opposite to pay your respects at the shrine to another revered figure, the Argentine footballer Diego Maradona.

If you're visiting at the weekend, find time to visit the lovely Cappella

San Domenico Maggiore

del Monte di Pietà, with a seventeenth-century frescoed ceiling and statues by Pietro Bernini on its facade. It's hidden away inside the Banca di Napoli at Via San Biagio dei Librai 114, and only open on Saturdays, Sunday and holiday afternoons.

A little further along, turn left into **Via San Gregorio Armeno ❻**. This narrow side street is entirely dedicated to the Neapolitan obsession with *presepi* – Christmas cribs. Stalls piled high with carved crib figurines, hand-crafted backdrops complete with ruins, trees and water features, fairy lights and baubles, lotto game boards and priapic good-luck charms spill out on to the street. Amongst the shepherds and wise men, look out for the modern-day heroes and villains, Barack Obama, Donald Trump, Silvio Berlusconi, Pope Francis and David Beckham among them.

If you reach the **church and convent of San Gregorio Armeno ❼** (Via di San Gregorio Armeno 1; www.suorecrocifisseadoratrici. org; free) before it closes, pop in to admire the interior, which is a riot of Baroque ornamentation, featuring frescoes by Luca Giordano.

San Lorenzo Maggiore

At the top of the street is the church of **San Lorenzo Maggiore ❽** (www.laneapolissotterrata.it; charge), another Angevin commission. Parts of the church, including the facade,

Neapolitan *presepi*

No Neapolitan household would be complete without its *presepe* (crib) at Christmas, but in Naples, the Nativity scene is as crowded as the city streets, with an exuberant cast of extras – children, musicians, peasants, farmers, dogs and chickens – rubbing shoulders with the usual shepherds, kings and angels. Figurine carving is still considered an art form and even if you're not in Naples at Christmas time, you'll find plenty of opportunities to admire it. The artisans in Via Gregorio Armeno do a roaring trade, and many of the larger churches display *presepi* year-round, each with their own cast of Neapolitan characters, usually depicted with unforgiving realism, in contrast to the delicate execution of the saints and angels. Don't miss the wonderful examples in Santa Chiara and the San Martino monastery.

were rebuilt in the eighteenth century, but most of the interior has been restored to its Gothic original. Skirting the altar is a magnificent semicircular ribbed vault. Sections of glass in the transept floor reveal the remains of a Roman mosaic.

To see more of the Greco-Roman city that lies beneath, head down the steps to the **archaeological site** where a section of the old Greco-

San Gregorio Armeno   San Lorenzo Maggiore

Roman road has been excavated. It led to the forum or *agora*, still buried in the foundations of San Paolo church. Works have exposed the city treasure house *(aerarium)*, a dyer's *(fullonica)*, a laundry *(lavanderia)* and Roman market *(macellum)*.

Via dei Tribunali

You are now on **Via dei Tribunali** (also known as the Decumano Maggiore), which arrows from Piazza Bellini to the Castel Capuano, and is as lively as Spaccanapoli, with the same dawn-to-dusk exuberance. Its abundance of excellent pizzerias makes Via dei Tribunali a good place to break for lunch; **Di Matteo**, see ③, is one of the best.

Piazza dei Girolamini

Continuing east to **Piazza dei Girolamini** ❾, you'll come across some examples of the age-old local *rigattiere* (bric-a-brac) trade, with shops selling all manner of junk (or treasure, depending on your point of view), from Communion goblets to broken accordions and fragments of antique statuary – a good place to hunt for quirky souvenirs.

Pio Monte della Misericordia

Cross busy Via Duomo and continue on Via dei Tribunali for the small church and picture gallery of **Pio Monte della Misericordia** ❿ (www.piomontedellamisericordia.

it; charge), famous for Caravaggio's immense altarpiece, the *Seven Acts of Mercy* (1607). The upstairs picture gallery displays works by some of the leading lights of Neapolitan Baroque: Luca Giordano, Massimo Stanzione and Giuseppe Ribera.

The Duomo

Back on Via Duomo, walk uphill to reach the **Duomo** ⓫ (www.campania.info; free), whose ungainly neo-Gothic facade conceals a fine medieval building. The main attraction of the Baroque interior, in the **Cappella di San Gennaro**, is a precious silver bust containing phials of the blood of the city's patron saint. Three times a year (the Saturday before the first Sunday in May, 19 September, and 16 December), devotees flock to the Duomo to witness the liquefying of San Gennaro's dried blood. If the 'miracle' fails to occur, the superstitious say disaster will strike.

The chapel glitters with more silver busts of saints, an exquisite silver altar in relief and a gilded bronze gate by Cosimo Fanzago. Access to the baptistry (550 AD) and the Greek and Roman remains of previous buildings on the site is from the left-hand nave. The next-door **Museo del Tesoro di San Gennaro** (www.tesorosangennaro.it; charge) features paintings, silverware and ex-votos dedicated to the saint.

Via dei Tribunali flower shop

Opposite the Duomo, and reached through a lovely cloister planted with lemon trees, the small **Quadreria dei Girolamini** 🔢 (Via Duomo 142; www.bibliotecadeigirolamini. beniculturali.it/la-quadreria; currently undergoing restoration) has fine paintings from the sixteenth to the eighteenth centuries.

M.A.D.RE

Further up Via Duomo, turn right on to Via Settembrini for Naples' key collection of modern art: the Museo d'Arte Contemporanea Donna Regina, or **M.A.D.RE** 🔢 (www.madre napoli.it; charge; closed Tues). On the first floor are site-specific works by artists such as Anish Kapoor and Jeff Koons; look out also for Jannis Kounellis' gigantic anchor and Rebecca Horn's unsettling *Spiriti*, with swivelling mirrors concealing ranks of skulls, set to eerie music.

On the second floor is an impressive collection of works by contemporary greats on long-term loan – Andy Warhol, Jasper Johns and Damien Hirst among them. The complex also includes the finely restored fourteenth-century church of Santa Maria Donnaregina Vecchia, used for temporary exhibitions.

It's not signposted, but you can ask the staff at M.A.D.RE to show you to the roof terrace, where Mimmo Paladino's *Cavallo* ('Horse') sculpture lords it over the city below.

San Paolo Maggiore

Backtrack to Via dei Tribunali. About halfway along is the imposing church of **San Paolo Maggiore** 🔢, built in the sixteenth century on the site of a temple to Castor and Pollux.

Napoli Sotterranea

Next door is the entrance to **Napoli Sotterranea** 🔢 (www.napoli sotterranea.org; 90 min guided tours only, available daily in English; charge), a fascinating journey through underground Naples. Steps lead 40m (131ft) underground to the tunnels and chambers of the vast Greco-Roman aqueduct that supplied the city with its water until the cholera epidemic of 1884. Sections of the disused aqueduct were used as shelters during the heavy Allied bombardments of World War II. Claustrophobics beware – to reach one chamber you have to squeeze through some very narrow tunnels, lighting your way with a candle – but there's no better place to get a feel for the city's multi-layered history.

Santa Maria delle Anime del Purgatorio ad Arco

On the last stretch of Via dei Tribunali, the bronze skulls on the railings outside the seventeenth-century church of **Santa Maria delle Anime del Purgatorio ad Arco** 🔢 (www.purgatorioadarco. it; free) indicate that this was no

Duomo paintings   Scooter life

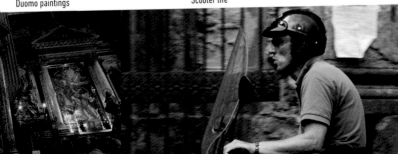

Food and Drink

1 Gay Odin

Via Benedetto Croce 61;
www.gay-odin.it; €
This historic chocolatier and *gelateria* has been keeping sweet-toothed Neapolitans happy for over a century. Now with branches all over the city, it's a wonderful place to shop for edible souvenirs – the chocolates are delicious and the gourmet ice creams are just as tempting.

2 Scaturchio

Piazza San Domenico Maggiore 19;
www.scaturchio.it; €
This long-established café not only serves an excellent cappuccino but is a great place to sample the classic Neapolitan sweets – *babà*, *sfogliatelle* and *pastiera*. The *ministeriali* – delectable coin-shaped chocolates stamped with the name of the bar's founder, Giovanni Scaturchio – look almost too good to eat.

3 Di Matteo

Via dei Tribunali 94;
www.pizzeriadimatteo.it; €
Whether or not its claim to have invented the pizza margherita (on 4 April 1936, apparently) is to be believed, Di Matteo is the archetypal Neapolitan pizzeria: rowdy, chaotic and very, very cheap. Head upstairs to soak up the atmosphere and (appetite permitting) go for the house speciality, *ripieno fritto* (fried calzone).

4 Caffè letterario Intra Moenia

Piazza Bellini 70; www.intramoenia.it; €
With its prime position on pretty Piazza Bellini, this café-bookshop is a popular spot throughout the day for drinks, snacks and light meals such as omelettes, sandwiches and salads, but it comes into its own at *aperitivo* hour, when the tables on the plant-filled terrace are in high demand. Live music on Wednesdays at 9.30pm.

ordinary church. It was long used for the worship of the dead, a practice officially forbidden by the Vatican, and the hypogeum still contains a pile of venerated bones.

Piazza Bellini

At Piazza Miraglia, Via dei Tribunali becomes Via San Pietro a Maiella, and passes the Gothic church of San Pietro a Maiella and the **Conservatorio di Musica**, with a lovely courtyard where the strains of students practising their instruments sounds like an orchestra tuning up; ask at the desk about performances in the recital hall. Turn right into leafy **Piazza Bellini** 🕗 and peer down at the section of Greco-Roman wall in the middle, before settling down to a well-deserved *aperitivo* on the shady terrace of **Intra Moenia**, see 4.

Leafy Piazza Bellini

WALK 2
Royal Naples

A full-day tour revealing Naples' monumental side. Marvel at the residences that were the hub of the Italian monarchy for over a thousand years, before joining the locals in a traditional seafront stroll.

> **DISTANCE:** 5km (3 miles)
> **TIME:** A full day
> **START:** Castel Nuovo
> **END:** Via Chiaia
> **POINTS TO NOTE:** The R2 bus runs from Piazza Garibaldi to Piazza Municipio. If possible, take this tour on a Sunday to join the Neapolitans out for their traditional weekly constitutional.

At the city's port, ferries and hydrofoils that shuttle commuters and day-trippers up and down the coast and across to the islands jostle for space with cruise and container ships. Standing guard over the port on traffic-choked Piazza Municipio is the Castel Nuovo (also known as the Maschio Angioino), the starting point of this tour.

Castel Nuovo

The Castel Nuovo ❶

(www.campaniartecard.it: charge) was called the 'new castle' to distinguish it from its predecessors, the Castel Capuano and Castel dell'Ovo. Built for Charles I of Anjou in 1279, the Angevin castle became a centre of culture, attracting writers and artists, including Giotto, whose frescoes in the chapel and main hall are barely visible today. The Angevins were ousted by the Aragonese in 1443, and the castle was reconstructed under Alfonso I.

The interior

Sandwiched between two of the five cylindrical towers, the gleaming Renaissance **Triumphal Arch** is a testament to the cultural renewal of Naples by the House of Aragon. The doors depict the victory of Aragonese over Angevins; these are replicas of the original doors, which can be seen inside the museum, complete with embedded cannonball. The central relief panel above the entrance arch shows Alfonso's triumphant entry into the city.

Across the courtyard, the **Palatine Chapel** is all that remains of the original thirteenth-century structure, and is now part of the **Museo Civico**, which displays mainly Neapolitan

Castel Nuovo

paintings, sculptures and bronzes from the eighteenth to the twentieth centuries over three floors. Don't miss the stately **Hall of the Barons**, with its spectacular rib-vaulted ceiling that soars to a height of 28m (92ft). Named after a group of rebellious noblemen executed here by King Ferdinand I for plotting his murder, it is now more prosaically used for city council meetings.

According to legend, a crocodile was shipped in from Egypt to devour errant prisoners in the castle dungeon and

Paintings adorn the walls at the Palazzo Reale

the taxidermized animal was displayed across the triumphal arch of the castle for many centuries. Recent DNA studies carried out on the remains have proven its provenance is indeed Egypt and that it dates from some time between the thirteenth and fifteenth centuries. Whether it is more plausible that it was a gift that arrived in its stuffed state is for visitors to decide.

Teatro San Carlo

Turn left out of Castel Nuovo and walk along Via Vittorio Emanuele to Via San Carlo and Piazza Trieste e Trento. Just before the square on your left is the **Teatro San Carlo** ❷ (www.teatrosancarlo. it; tours daily according to theatre schedule; charge), Italy's largest and oldest opera house, predating the Scala in Milan by forty years. Commissioned by Charles of Bourbon in 1737 and completed in just eight months, it quickly became one of the most important social venues in eighteenth-century Naples – and the stage of many a scandalous liaison. The plush six-tiered auditorium, all red velvet and gold stucco, can seat up to three thousand people. Tickets are not cheap, but watching a performance here is a rare treat. For more on the theatre's history, drop in on its state-of-the-art archive and museum, Memus which features a 3D virtual gallery and has a bookshop.

Via Toledo and the Quartieri Spagnoli

On the opposite side of Via San Carlo, underneath the arcade, is the main entrance to the **Galleria Umberto I** ❸. The magnificent glass-roofed gallery, built in 1890, is lined with smart shops and cafés; the western exit brings you out on to **Via Toledo** ❹, Naples' main shopping thoroughfare.

The grid of streets leading west off Via Toledo make up the **Quartieri Spagnoli** ❺ (Spanish Quarter). Built to house the Spanish military, the cramped dwellings later became home to Naples' working classes. The labyrinth of narrow streets, festooned with lines of washing, have become an evocative symbol of inner-city Naples.

Piazza Plebiscito

You will have spotted the traffic-free, semicircular Piazza Plebiscito by now. Before heading over there, stop for a coffee at **Caffè Gambrinus**, see ❶. In 1994, **Piazza Plebiscito** – the 'People's Square' – was reclaimed by the people. Until then, this magnificent square had been used as a car park, but was cleared of traffic as part of a citywide clean-up in the 1990s. The piazza is embraced by the twin arcades of **San Francesco di Paola**, an imposing neoclassical church inspired by the Pantheon in Rome. The two equestrian statues gracing the square commemorate the two Bourbon

WALK 2   PIAZZA PLEBISCITO

The grand interior of the Palazzo Reale

kings, Ferdinand I and Charles III; both were sculpted by Canova.

Palazzo Reale

Opposite the church, the **Palazzo Reale** ❻ (Piazza Plebiscito 1; www.palazzorealedinapoli.it: charge) is the highlight of this tour. Built in the middle of the sixteenth century, its design was tweaked on numerous occasions over the centuries, each ruler leaving his mark. The statues along the facade – the eight dynasties that ruled Naples from Roger the Norman to Victor Emmanuel of Savoy – present a potted history of the city.

Inside, a double staircase ascends to the **royal apartments**, resplendent with Baroque and neoclassical paintings, sculpture, tapestries and porcelain. The highlights are the **Court Theatre** (1768) and the **Royal Chapel**, which has a magnificent altar by Lazzari (1674), master of Neapolitan Baroque decoration, and a vast *presepe* (Christmas crib). The palace is also home to the **Biblioteca Nazionale** di Napoli (www.bnnonline.it) its collection of books and manuscripts includes some two thousand parchments from Herculaneum. The palace's beautifully restored hanging gardens offer marvellous views stretching over the gulf to Vesuvius to Capri. Before leaving, anyone interested in theatre or opera could check out Memus, the Teatro San

Carlo's museum, shop and archive with an exhibition space for props and costumes and a virtual reality gallery.

Santa Lucia

Exit the square on Via Cesario Console, then turn right into **Via Santa Lucia** ❼, which cuts through the old fishermen's quarter and leads down to the sea. Rising above it to the right is the **Pizzofalcone** hill, site of the Greek settlement of Parthenope that predated Neapolis by three centuries.

Luxury hotels hog all the best views along Via Partenope, the road that skirts the bay. Nestled in the tiny harbour at the foot of the castle is the **Borgo Marinaro** ❽, an atmospheric enclave of seafood restaurants, romantically candlelit after dark, or a stunning spot for lunch, surrounded by bobbing fishing boats. Stop at La Scialuppa, see ❷, for fish.

Castel dell'Ovo

The **Castel dell'Ovo** ❾ (www.campaniartecard.it; free) is the oldest castle in Naples. It occupies a tiny islet named Megaris by the Greeks, who used it as a harbour.

The original fortress was built by the Aragonese in the twelfth century, but most of the present structure dates from the early sixteenth century, when the citadel was rebuilt following its near destruction by the Spanish. Today, the castle is used to

Castel dell'Ovo

Food and Drink

① Caffè Gambrinus
Via Chiaia 1–2; tel: 081-417 582;
http://grancaffegambrinus.com; €
This elegant Art Nouveau café, decked
out with marble and chandeliers,
dates from 1860. Once a popular haunt
of artists, writers and politicians,
it's now a time-honoured favourite
for coffee and pastries during the
day, early-evening *aperitivi* and
pre-clubbing pick-me-ups.

② La Scialuppa
Piazzetta Marinari 5;
www.lascialuppa.net; €€€
Now in its fifth generation, bustling
La Scialuppa is a great place for a
waterfront lunch of seafood pasta
or a plate of peppered mussels.
Very popular, so catching a
waiter's eye is not always easy.

③ Enoteca Belledonne
Via Belledonne a Chiaia 18;
www.enotecabelledonne.eu; €
The early-evening crowds at this
popular wine bar shun the tables
in favour of the cobbled street
outside. Come between 7pm and
10pm or after midnight for the best
atmosphere – or outside of these
times if you're after a quiet drink.

host cultural events and exhibitions,
but the real appeal is exploring the
battlements, gazing at the views.

According to legend, buried in the
rock beneath the Castel dell'Ovo lies
an ancient egg *(uovo)*, which holds
the fate of the city within its shell.
The Roman poet Virgil, believed
to possess powers of divination,
prophesied that if the egg broke,
catastrophe would befall the city.

The Lungomare

The broad stretch of road that sweeps
around the bay from the castle, past
the Villa Comunale to Mergellina,
is punctuated at each end by a
seventeenth-century fountain. A stroll
along the traffic-free seafront, or
Lungomare ⑩, with an ice cream in
hand, is a Neapolitan Sunday ritual.

Chiaia

Continue along Via Partenope until
you reach the park, then turn right
into **Piazza Vittoria ⑪** and follow
boutique-lined Via Calabritto to
Piazza dei Martiri ⑫, the epicentre
of chichi Chiaia. Take the next
left on to Via Alabardieri to reach
Enoteca Belledonne, see ③, before
wandering back to Piazza Plebiscito
along pedestrianised **Via Chiaia ⑬**,
a favourite spot for a *passeggiata*.
favoured by Naples' best-dressed
for their evening *passeggiata*.

Via Chiaia balcony

The fortress-island

WALK 3
Chiaia and Vomero

A full day exploring the well-heeled and pleasantly airy districts of Chiaia, with its chichi boutiques, and Vomero, with its spacious avenues and knockout views, culminating in a stroll along the seafront to lively Mergellina.

DISTANCE: 6km (3.75 miles)
TIME: A full day
START: Piazza dei Martiri
END: Mergellina
POINTS TO NOTE: This is a good route for children. City Sightseeing bus #B run throughout year from Piazza Municipio to Castel Sant'Elmo, stopping at Chiaia and Piazza Vanvitelli in Vomero en route (www.napoli.city-sightseeing.it).

Chiaia became fashionable in the nineteenth century and it remains a pocket of privilege from which its impeccably attired residents rarely stray. The Vomero hill above was just a sleepy village until the turn of the century. The building of elegant neo-Renaissance *palazzi* attracted wealthy Neapolitans, but after World War II, unregulated building covered most of the hill with modern blocks. Traces of its past endure, however, in a few handsome old buildings.

Chiaia

Start at **Piazza dei Martiri** ❶, Chiaia's lively hub. Head north out of the square, veering left into **Via G. Filangieri**, which becomes Via dei Mille. Both streets are lined with exclusive shops and designer boutiques, with *palazzi* in between.

At Via dei Mille 60, the **Palazzo delle Arti di Napoli** ❷ (www.comune.napoli.it/pan-palazzodelleartinapoli; charge), or PAN for short, is a must for contemporary-art lovers. Exhibitions range from sculpture to photography to comics – and there's a great shop too.

The network of streets between this stretch and the Riviera di Chiaia yields more boutiques – Via della Cavallerizza and Via Poerio are particularly good. Via dei Mille runs into Via Vittoria Colonna, which ends at **Piazza Amedeo** ❸. The road to the right of the metro station here leads to the **funicular** ❹, which whisks you up to Vomero; get off at the last stop, **Cimarosa** ❺.

Riviera di Chiaia

Villa Floridiana

Turn left out of the funicular station and walk along Via Cimarosa until you reach the **Villa Floridiana** ⑥. Bench-lined paths wind past densely planted shrubbery, opening out on to a lawn – a favourite local picnic spot – and the Villa Floridiana. Once described as a 'Baroque chocolate box with neoclassical touches', it was a

An exhibit at the National Ceramic Museum

Villa Floridiana

wedding present from King Ferdinand I to his wife, Lucia Migliaccio.

Museo Nazionale di Ceramica

The villa now houses the **Museo Nazionale della Ceramica Duca di Martina** ❼ (www.coopculture.it; charge)with one of Italy's finest collections of fine china, including eighteenth-century porcelain from Meissen, Limoges, Sèvres and nearby Capodimonte, and an exceptional oriental collection. Before leaving Villa Floridiana, walk round the back through the gardens to the viewing platform at the bottom, which offers panoramic views of the city and the bay.

Back at the park gates, turn right onto Via Cimarosa and stop at **Acunzo**, see ❶, for lunch. Backtrack to the funicular and take Via Bernini, leading off it, to **Piazza Vanvitelli** ❽.

Castel Sant'Elmo

Take Via Alessandro Scarlatti, which leads off Piazza Vanvitelli to the right, climbing the two flights of steps up to the funicular station. Follow the road round to the right for the hulking **Castel Sant'Elmo** ❾ (entrance at Via Tito Angelini 20; www.coopculture.it; charge). Construction of the fortress was begun in 1329 by Robert of Anjou; in the mid-sixteenth century, Spanish viceroy Don Pedro de Toledo added the six-pointed star shape, making the castle

virtually impregnable. But in 1587 disaster struck when an explosion in the powder magazine all but destroyed it. The castle was gradually rebuilt and for many years served as a dungeon. Today the interior holds the **Museo del Novecento**, displaying local art from 1910 to 1980; more compelling is the staggering 360-degree view of the city from its battlements.

Back at the gate, turn right to continue the walk.

San Martino Monastery

Sharing the castle's hilltop perch is the **San Martino Monastery** ❿ (Certosa di San Martino, Largo San Martino 8; www.coopculture.it; charge), founded in 1325 but redesigned in the seventeenth century.

Cosimo Fanzago expanded the original **Angevin church**, giving it a Baroque makeover. He added a new facade and had the interior decorated with marble and paintings by the masters of Neapolitan Baroque.

A door at the back of the church leads to the **sacristy and chapter room**, with inlaid walnut panelling. You emerge from these sombre rooms into the bright **Chiostro Grande**, enclosed by a 64-column arcade of grey and white marble and a monks' graveyard, watched over by an eerie set of skulls ranged along a balustrade.

The **art gallery** is spread across two floors, its rooms facing on to

View from Castel Sant'Elmo

the cloister on one side and offering more fantastic views of Naples on the other. Most of the seventeenth - and eighteenth-century works are housed in the former prior's quarters. Among the fine maps and landscapes, look out for the earliest pictorial record of Naples, the **Tavola Strozzi** (1465), showing the original monastery atop Vomero hill.

Backtrack to the Cimarosa funicular and return to Chiaia.

Villa Pignatelli

From Piazza Amadeo, take Via Vittoria Colonna and turn right down the steps for **Museo Pignatelli** ⑪ (Via della Riviera di Chiaia 200; www.coopculture.it; charge). The neoclassical villa was built in 1826 for Ferdinand Acton, son of Ferdinand IV's prime minister. It was bought in 1841 by the Rothschilds, who sold it to the noble Pignatelli Cortes family. As well as elaborate nineteenth century furniture, porcelain and gilded bronze, there is a small museum of photography and, in the stables, a collection of antique carriages.

Villa Comunale

Crossing traffic-choked Riviera di Chiaia to the **Villa Comunale** ⑫, it's hard to imagine a time when this was a peaceful residential area. King Ferdinand IV cleared a block of buildings along here to turn his

favourite strolling ground into a public park filled with exotic plants.

The **Stazione Zoologica Acquario** ⑬ (www.szn.it; charge) is Europe's oldest aquarium: built in 1874, it still contains the original 23 tanks.

Mergellina

Exit the park and follow Via Caracciolo west along the seafront to the port of **Mergellina** ⑭. On the opposite side of the marina is a line-up of kiosks – or 'chalets' – selling drinks and snacks; these include **Chalet Ciro**, see ②.

Opulent Villa Pignatelli

The port of Mergellina

WALK 4
The Catacombs and Museums

This route explores the artistic and archaeological treasures of Naples' top two museums, and takes in some more offbeat sights en route, notably one of the area's subterranean cemeteries and the engagingly non-touristy district of La Sanità.

DISTANCE: 2.5km (1.5 miles)
TIME: A full day
START: Museo di Capodimonte
END: Museo Archeologico Nazionale
POINTS TO NOTE: To get to the Museo di Capodimonte take bus R4 or C63 from the port or Piazza Dante, or bus 178 or 168 from Piazza Museo. You will need at least three hours for each museum, but the tour can be split up. Take an extra layer of clothing for the catacombs as they can be chilly, and watch your belongings in La Sanità.

When the noise and chaos of the city get too much for you, head for the Museo di Capodimonte and its tranquil gardens and the Museo Archeologico. Between the two are a number of lesser-known sights that are rewarding in their own way, namely the fascinating Catacombs of San Gaudioso and the workaday district of La Sanità.

Museo di Capodimonte

The **Museo di Capodimonte** ❶ (www.capodimonte.cultura.gov.it; charge), one of Italy's finest art museums, sits in the hilltop haven of Capodimonte, in its own park. When he became king, Charles III of Bourbon gathered all the artworks he had inherited from his mother, Elisabetta Farnese, to Naples. The problem was where to house them. While on one of his hunting trips, the king decided that the hill to the north of the city, with its game-filled woods, was the perfect site for a hunting lodge and royal residence that would double as a museum for his precious collection. Building began in 1738, but progress was slow: the three-storey palace took one hundred years to complete.

The core Farnese collection, rich in Renaissance art, was augmented by the Bourbon collection and subsequent acquisitions, many from churches and convents in the area. The collection now ranges Byzantine to contemporary.

The Museo di Capodimonte

early works – Masaccio's *Crucifixion*, a Botticelli Madonna and Filippino Lippi's *Annunciation and Saints* – but the sixteenth-century paintings are the cream of the crop. Highlights include *Antea* by Parmigianino, the portrait of an elegantly dressed young woman thought to be the artist's lover, and the monumental canvases by the Carraccis. The influence of Michelangelo is evident in the sculpted figures of Annibale Carracci's *Pietà* and in his Hercules at the Crossroads. Raphael is a dominant presence with his portraits of *Leo X and Two Cardinals* and *Cardinal Alessandro Farnese*. Pride of place is given to Titian's *Danaë*, which represents the mythical love scene from Ovid's *Metamorphoses* in which Zeus disguises himself as a shower of gold in order to seduce Danaë, daughter of the king of Argos. In the same room is *El Soflon*

Farnese Gallery

The visit begins with the **Farnese Gallery** on the first floor. The collection features some important

The Farnese Gallery

by El Greco, a mesmerising study of young boy blowing on a burning coal.

Galleria delle Cose Rare

The **Galleria delle Cose Rare** contains a sparkling display of rare and precious objects that once graced the Farnese palaces. The rooms beyond are taken up by Flemish paintings, mostly acquired by the Bourbons at the beginning of the seventeenth century, a mix of earthy, pastoral scenes and still lifes.

Royal apartments

Before heading up to the second floor, wander through the ornate **Royal Apartments** and marvel at the ballroom with its giant chandelier, and the Porcelain Parlour of Queen Maria Amalia, lined with over three thousand tiles made in King Charles's porcelain factory.

Second floor

The second floor is given over to Neapolitan art from the thirteenth to the eighteenth centuries. Among the early works is Simone Martini's *San Ludovico di Tolosa*, a masterpiece of Italian Gothic art from San Lorenzo Maggiore. Central to the seventeenth-century works in the collection are the Caravaggio canvases, in particular the *Flagellation*, which was transferred from San Domenico Maggiore. This influential painting heralded a golden age of Neapolitan art, whose leading

lights were Mattia Preti, Giuseppe de Ribera, Battistello Caracciolo and Luca Giordano, all represented. Don't miss the monumental d'Avalos tapestries, made in Brussels for the Habsburg emperor Charles V, to commemorate his victory over the French in the Battle of Pavia.

The gallery's modern-art collection starts on the second floor with Alberto Burri's imposing *Grande Cretto Nero*.

Third floor

The third floor and part of the former attics, closed for restoration (and to improve energy efficiency) until 2025, are dedicated to modern and contemporary art. Don't miss Andy Warhol's iconic *Vesuvius*. Before leaving, browse in the prints and drawings gallery on the ground floor. Its 27,500-strong collection includes cartoons by Raphael and Michelangelo, and prints by, among others, Dürer and Rembrandt.

There's more contemporary art in the **Sala Causa**, off the courtyard, which holds big-name temporary exhibitions.

Parco di Capodimonte

Revive yourself with a coffee in the courtyard café and then take a stroll around the **Parco di Capodimonte**. The gardens were laid out in 1742 by architect Sanfelice, whose designs were influenced both by the formal French style and the Romantic English style. Sanfelice was also commissioned to

Caravaggio's 'Flagellation'

build the royal porcelain factory, which turned out top-quality porcelain until Charles dismantled the operation and transferred it, workers and all, to Spain when he returned there in 1759.

Take bus C63, 178 or 2M from almost opposite the entrance to the park and get off at the first stop after you pass the green-and-yellow tiled cupola on your left (or it's a 25-minute walk down the twisting road). Here you'll find a lift *(ascensore)* down to the district of La Sanità and, beneath the church of Santa Maria della Sanità, the Catacombs of San Gaudioso.

Catacombe di San Gaudioso

The area beneath the park and down towards La Sanità is honeycombed with catacombs, which can be visited.

First tunnelled out of the rock by the Ancient Romans, who used them as water cisterns, the **Catacombe di San Gaudioso ❷** (Piazza della Sanità 14; www.catacombedinapoli.it; charge) were used as Christian burial sites from the fifth century onwards. Through the musty gloom you can still make out remnants of fifth - and sixth-century mosaics and faded frescoes: look out for the Christian symbols of the lamb, the peacock, and the bunch of grapes.

Your catacombs ticket also gets you entry to the two-level Catacombe di San Gennaro, at Via Tondo di Capodimonte 13, which are embellished with second-century frescoes.

La Sanità

Back above ground, explore **La Sanità**, one of Naples' most characterful districts: untouched by tourism, this appealingly rowdy network of streets is a great place to absorb yourself in the sights and sounds of the city. Follow **Via della Sanità ❸** from the church. Full of the chaotic energy that characterises Naples and buzzing at all hours, this stretch offers as authentic a slice of Neapolitan life as you'll find anywhere in the city. The area is peppered with Catholic shrines – stop at Traversa Lammatari and look to your right for a typically overblown example.

Via delle Vergini

Just before the road veers left, peek into the courtyard of the **Palazzo Sanfelice ❹** to your right to admire its magnificent – though sadly dilapidated – double staircases. Via della Sanità merges with **Via delle Vergini ❺**, site of a colourful local market (daily 8am–8pm), selling everything from flowers to frying pans. No. 19, **Palazzo dello Spagnuolo ❻**, holds another impressive double staircase, this one restored. A small museum dedicated to Totò, veteran comic actor and the area's most famous son is planned on the top floor.

Just off Via delle Vergini, on the Via Fuori Porta San Gennaro 13/14, you can stop for lunch at **La Campagnola**, see ❶, or, further

Catacomb fresco

Palazzo Sanfelice

down at Piazza Cavour, have a snack at **Mignone**, see ❷, before moving on to the Museo Archeologico.

Museo Archeologico

At the far end of Piazza Cavour, the **Museo Archeologico Nazionale** ❼ (National Archeological Museum; Piazza Museo 19; www.mann-napoli.it or www.coopculture.it; charge) is an unparalleled collection of Greek and Roman artefacts. The museum occupies a hulking red *palazzo* on the northern outskirts of the *centro storico*. Originally the seat of Naples University, the seventeenth-century building was requisitioned in 1777 by Ferdinand IV to house the Farnese collection bequeathed to him by his father, Charles III of Bourbon. Charles's mother came from the aristocratic Farnese family whose members had assembled a vast collection of antique and contemporary art. Ferdinand wanted to gather as much of the scattered collection as he could under one roof with the aim of establishing a 'temple of wisdom and knowledge'.

Farnese collection

The Farnese collection of antiquities is spread across the ground floor. Many of the sculptures are in fact Roman copies of Greek masterpieces. The Farnese *Hercules* in the main gallery is a first-rate copy of a statue by the Greek master Lysippus. At the opposite end stands the *Farnese Bull* (*c.*200 BC), a monumental sculpture carved from a single block of marble. It depicts the death of Dirce, tied to a bull by Antiope's sons for the attempted murder of their mother. Both statues come from the Baths of Caracalla in Rome. Other highlights are the *Aphrodite Callipige*, admiring the reflection of her curvaceous rear; the bronze and alabaster *Artemis of Ephesus*; and the *Tyrannicides*, a copy of a fourth-century Greek original.

Leading off the main gallery is a room full of incised gems and intricate cameos, while in the basement is the museum's small Egyptian collection, part of which came from the Borgia family (closed for restoration at the time of writing).

Mosaics collection

The mezzanine floor is shared between a 200,000-strong coin collection on one side, and Roman mosaics and the 'secret room' of Pompeiian erotica on the other. The finest mosaics come from the houses of wealthy Pompeiians, most notably the House of the Faun (named after the lovely bronze sculpture of a dancing faun, displayed on the first floor). The undisputed masterpiece here is the mosaic of the Battle of Issus, depicting Alexander the Great's victory over the Persian king Darius. Animals were a favourite theme and there are realistic portrayals of cats and dogs, exotic creatures from the Nile and marine life.

Museo Archeologico lion

Gabinetto Segreto

The so-called **Gabinetto Segreto** is the biggest draw; in high season, put your name on the list when you buy your entrance ticket to minimise waiting time. Until recently, the statuettes, reliefs, mosaics and frescoes displayed here were deemed too pornographic for public viewing; the entrance to the secret room is still manned to prevent under-12s from going in. The explicit images of sexual antics between men, women, nymphs, satyrs and, in one case, a god and a goat, will leave you in no doubt as to the Roman taste for eroticism. Phalluses abound in every shape and form; as well as symbolising virility and fertility, they were used as good-luck charms to ward off the evil eye.

First floor

All the rooms on the first floor lead off the central **Salone Meridiana**, a vast hall decorated with frescoes and paintings glorifying the Bourbon. Set into the floor of the Salone Meridiana is a meridian line decorated at calculated intervals with signs of the zodiac. At midday a shaft of light falls from a hole in the top right-hand corner of the room and hits the sign that corresponds to the time of year. Most of this floor is dedicated to the Vesuvian paintings, as well as items from Paestum and other sites of Magna Grecia. Highlights also include the 118-piece silver collection

---

Food and Drink

① La Campagnola
Via Fuori Porta San Gennaro 13/14 ; tel: 081- 457 663; €
The décor here is simple, but this busy trattoria-pizzeria is hugely popular and well-priced. The *calzone* are excellent, featuring four types of cheese. Also worth a try is the pasta with potato and provola cheese.

② Mignone
Piazza Cavour 145; tel: 081-293 074; €
This hole-in-the-wall *pasticceria* has all the Neapolitan classics – *babà, pastiera, ogliatelle* – as well as gourmet chocolates. The rum babà is a legend – attested by frequent queues. Perfect for a sugar hit before you tackle the Museo Archeologico.

---

from the Casa del Menandro, part of a hoard found in a wooden chest together with gold jewellery, precious stones and silver and gold coins; the famous Blue Vase, a glass-cameo amphora from Pompeii; and a series of rooms containing bronze statues and a wealth of other finds from the **Villa dei Papiri** in Herculaneum.

If the day's sightseeing has given you a healthy appetite, head to **Osteria Da Carmela** (see page 99), a short stroll south along Via Santa Maria di Costantinopoli.

WALK 4   MUSEO ARCHEOLOGICO

Museo Archeologico sculptures

TOUR 5
The Campi Flegrei

This tour covers the little-explored but fascinating Phlegraean Fields. Once mythologised by the ancients as the entrance to the Underworld, this area of geological quirks and archaeological wonders makes for a rewarding daytrip from Naples and is a good way to escape the crowds.

DISTANCE: 4km (2.5 miles) on foot and 20km (12.5 miles) by car/bus/train

TIME: A full day

START: Pozzuoli

END: Cuma

POINTS TO NOTE: The Campi Flegrei are well connected by public transport, and all major sights and attractions are served by buses and trains. By public transport, take a train from Naples' Montesanto station to Pozzuoli on the Cumana line or to Cuma on the Circumflegrea line. From the Lucrino stop (Cumana line) take a bus to Baia. EAV buses run from Báia and Bacoli to Cuma. By car, take the Tangenziale (ring road) west from Naples through Fuorigrotta; exits are marked. A boat service usually runs from Molo Beverello to the Campi Flegrei in summer; see www.ilmattino.it for the timetable. Ferries also run to Pozzuoli from Ischia and Procida (tours 11 and 12). Wear sturdy footwear and bring a picnic.

The area west of Naples, between Pozzuoli and Cuma, is known as the **Campi Flegrei** (Phlegraean Fields), from the Greek *fleguròs* meaning fire. Back in the eighth century BC, when the first Greek colonists settled in Cuma, the volcanic terrain bubbled and hissed with the activity of some forty craters. Its ghostly atmosphere led the ancients to believe this was the gateway of the dead, and inspired Virgil and Dante to create their vision of hell. But such sinister associations didn't deter the Romans, who were drawn by the fertile land, mild climate and hot springs, and built villas and spas along the coast.

By the first century AD, the Campi Flegrei was one of the empire's most fashionable resorts – a far cry from its neglected modern-day incarnation: the Greco-Roman ruins lie buried under a sea of concrete. Picturesque it isn't, but its steeped in ancient history and far off the tourist trail.

The Campi Flegrei is the caldera of a volcano officially classed as a supervolcano, which means that

Pozzuoli's Tempio di Serapide

it once had what is known as a supereruption (ejecting a terrifying 1000 cubic kilometres or more molten rock and gas). Although one of the most seismically active places in Europe – two thousand five hundred earthquakes were registered in autumn 2023 – experts doubt that an eruption is imminent, and the quakes are triggered by movements below the surface.

The Campania Artecard tourist passes, available for either three, or seven days, gives access to sights throughout Campania (the Napoli Artecard only covers the city). Alternatively, a joint Phlegraean Circuit ticket gives access to the Parco Archeologico delle Terme di Baia, the Sito Archeologico di Cumae, Museo Archeologico dei Campi Flegrei (in Baia) and the Anfiteatro Flavio (in Pozzuoli).

Pozzuoli

The starting point of this itinerary is the port of **Pozzuoli ❶**, which

Yachts moored in Pozzuoli harbour

has three claims to fame: its Greco-Roman remains, its active crater and its the birthplace of Sophia Loren. There's a lot to see so get here early.

Tempio di Serapide

The Cumana train drops you near the port. Turn right from the station to reach the first-century market, or **Tempio di Serapide**, on the seafront, which was submerged in water until 1985 when the effects of bradyseism – the rising and falling of land levels caused by volcanic activity – left it uncovered.

Rione Terra

Backtrack to the station and take Via G. De Fraia to your left to get to the centre, then turn left and walk up the hill for the **Rione Terra (charge)**. There's an ancient town, with remains of an Augustan temple, a bakery, a mill and slave lodgings. Now head back down to the station. (see page 99).

Anfiteatro Flavio

Bus 152 runs from the opposite side of the piazza from the station to the **Anfiteatro Flavio ②** (Via Terracciano 75; www.coopculture.it; charge). This well-preserved amphitheatre held forty thousand spectators and was the third largest in the ancient world.

Solfatara

Bus 152 continues uphill to the **Solfatara ③** (Via Solfatara 161; charge), an active

crater in a strikingly lunar landscape. At the time of writing activity was considered too intense to allow access to the public, but if it is deemed safe again, you can expect to feel the heat, smell the pungent sulphur and even see fumaroles, gas jets and bubbling mud.

Buses P9 and 152 run back down to the station, where you can take a train to Lucrino, then a bus to Báia. You could stop and have lunch first at Ristorante **Bobo**, see ①, or **Osteria DOC**, see ②.

Báia

Traces of an old Roman baths complex and adjacent temples are scattered along the **port of Báia ④**, but you need to stretch your imagination to see this nondescript town as the luxurious spa it was. Much of the ancient resort lies under the sea due to bradyseism. At weekends in summer, glass-bottomed boats ferry tourists to the ruined villas under the water (charge). Booking is essential (www.baiasommersa.it).

Castello di Báia

The road out of the port winds round to Báia's main attraction, the **Castello di Báia**, now the **Museo Archeologico dei Campi Flegrei ⑤** (www.coopculture.it; charge), sitting in splendid isolation at the tip of the headland, overlooking the Gulf of Pozzuoli. Built by the Aragonese, it was restructured by Don Pedro de Toledo after the 1538 eruption. Inside is an impressive collection of local

Bubbling Solfatara

Food and Drink

1 Bobo

Via Cristoforo Colombo 20, Pozzuoli, www.ristorantebobo.com; €€
Harbourside restaurant which does great fish and has an excellent wine list. Try the pasta with sea urchins or with mussels and zucchini, or a host of other great pasta and fish dishes. Not particularly cheap, but the perfect end to a morning at the market.

2 Giardini di Kyme

Via Montenuovo Licola Patria 131g, Pozzuoli, www.giardinidikyme.it; €€
Sit back with views over beautifully manicured lawns and the sea glinting in the distance to enjoy seafood, steak and antipasti platters alongside a fine Italian wine. Advance bookings required.

3 Osteria DOC

Corso Umberto 1 181, Pozzuoli, https://osteriadoc.eatbu.com; €€
This wine bar offers creative cuisine with seasonal specials (the menu changes monthly) and a choice of set menus. You'll usually find pasta dishes – lasagne, gnocchi – along with light dishes such as *frittate*, and ham, salami and cheese platters.

archaeological treasures, including sculptures found on the seabed and fragments of Roman moulds.

Buses run from Báia to Bacoli; ask the driver where to get off for the **Piscina Mirabilis** (www.piscina mirabilisbacoli.it). Tickets are available from Via Campi Elisi, 1, with visits possible Friday to Sunday (guided tours posisble). This immense cistern, carved out of the rock held enough water to supply the Roman fleet anchored at Miseno.

Cuma

From Bacoli or Báia get an EAV bus to the Cuma archaeological site ('Cuma Scavi'). From where the bus stops, walk up the hill past the **Archaeological Park**, containing remains of the ancient Roman bath complex.

The main site **Cuma 6** (www.coop culture.it; charge) is a little further up the hill. The first colony of Magna Grecia, it was founded in the eighth century BC by Greek traders based in Ischia. The finest sight is the Cave of the Sibyl, a long, echoing trapezoid corridor carved into the hill of the acropolis. Steps lead up to the ruins of the **Temple of Apollo** and, higher still, the **Temple of Jupiter**. It's worth the climb for the sweeping views.

Buses run from the site to Fusaro Cumana station, from where you can take a train back to Naples. Stop in **Giardini di Kyme**, see 3 for refreshments before you go

View from Castello di Báia

Cuma's Cave of the Sibyl

TOUR 6
Pompeii, Vesuvius and Herculaneum

Explore Pompeii, one of the world's most evocative ancient sites, followed by a visit to Vesuvius, the volcano that obliterated the town. Neighbouring Herculaneum – smaller and quieter – is, for many, the most rewarding site of all.

DISTANCE: 35km (21.75 miles) public transport and 11km (7 miles) on foot
TIME: A full day
START: Pompeii
END: Herculaneum
POINTS TO NOTE: Allow 2–3 hours for Pompeii minimum. Allow 3 hours for Vesuvius, and 1-2 hours for Hercolaneum. You can buy a single ticket for Pompeii, and the archaeological areas of Boscoreale, Oplontis and Stabiae, all linked by a free shuttle bus, the Pompeii Artebus. Circumvesuviana trains run along the Naples–Sorrento line to Pompeii Scavi-Villa dei Misteri station, and also on the Naples–Poggiomarino line to Pompei Santuario station. Vesuvius and Herculaneum can be reached from Ercolano Scavi station, on the Naples–Sorrento, Naples–Poggiomarino and Naples–Torre Annunziata lines. By car, take the A3 Naples–Salerno motorway; exit Pompei Ovest. From Pompeii to Vesuvius and Herculaneum, take the A3 towards Naples; exit Ercolano.

When Mount Vesuvius erupted some time in the autumn of,AD 79, it had barely murmured for eight hundred years, so the destruction it caused is all the more startling. Until recently, the date ascribed to the eruption was 24 August. However, the discovery of the date 24 October AD 79 graffitied on the wall of newly excavated house has thrown this into doubt. Archeologists also point out that the presence of braziers in many of the houses along with fragments of heavy clothing found on victims suggests that the weather was cold.

At about 1pm, Vesuvius began to spew ash and stone thousands of metres into the air. The volcanic debris rained down on Pompeii, a thriving Roman town with a population of 20,000, smothering its buildings and inhabitants in a thick blanket of ash. Herculaneum, a humbler town to the west with fewer five thousand fishermen, craftsmen and farmers, and a few Roman aristocrats who had holiday homes there, was only mildly affected at this

Exploring the remains

Pompeii

The entrance point to the ruins of **Pompeii** ❶ (www.pompeiisites. org) is ancient **Porta Marina Ⓐ**. Make sure you pick up a plan of the excavations, as well as a detailed map which will have timed itineraries depending on whether you have just a couple of hours or a whole day at your disposal. If you are planning

stage. Later that night, a scalding mixture of gas, ash and rock blasted Herculaneum; the town was then covered in a 20m (66ft) layer of mud.

Herculaneum was discovered by chance, in 1709, by a peasant digging a well; the first sections of Pompeii were unearthed by archaeologists of the Bourbon court of Charles III in 1748. The eruption effectively froze life in Pompeii as it was at the time, and the site has probably yielded more information about the ordinary life of Roman citizens during the imperial era than any other. Its unique importance made it an essential stop for Europeans on the Grand Tour, and has captured the imagination of visitors ever since.

In high season, the crowds at Pompeii can be overwhelming, and it is advisable to book online well in advance, and download the excellent maps which include an itinerary for wheelchair users and those of limited mobility.

Pompeii in peril

Coachloads of tourists walk Pompeii's cobbled streets on a daily basis, ogling its chipped mosaics and snapping its faded frescoes. But Pompeii is now at risk for a second time: relentless foot traffic and the effects of the wind and rain on exposed ancient stones are taking their toll, and despite the site's importance, lack of investment has meant that priceless relics have been neglected for years. After a series of collapses, the Italian government declared a state of emergency, and in 2013 work began on a 105 million euro makeover – focused on reducing the risk of exposure to the elements and restoring the site's priceless frescoes – in a bid to preserve what remains. The work was completed in October 2023.

Teatro Grande at Pompeii

on a full day, consider bringing a picnic as food options are limited.

The road leads through Porta Marina past the temples of Venus and Apollo and into the **Forum ❸**, the centre of public life. Straight ahead, the **Tempio di Giove ❹** (Temple of Jupiter) is silhouetted against the dramatic backdrop of Vesuvius. To the left, inside the old granary stores, are displayed stacks of terracotta storage jars and plaster casts of carbonised victims.

North of the Forum

In the grid of streets north of the Forum, between the ruins of roadside tavernas and ordinary dwellings, a number of well-preserved Patrician villas reveal how the other half lived. The houses of the wealthy were walled around the outside for privacy. Light came from the open courtyards (atria) and porticoed gardens (peristyles), around which the richly decorated rooms were arranged. Two of the best examples of Roman domestic architecture are the **Casa del Fauno ❹** (Via della Fortuna), named after the bronze statue of a dancing faun found here, and the nearby **Casa dei Vettii** (Vicolo dei Vettii), the home of rich wine merchants.

Villa dei Misteri fresco

Villa dei Misteri

Make your way to the **Porta di Ercolano** in the northwestern corner. It's a pleasant walk along the Via dei Sepolcri, flanked with ancient funerary monuments, to the **Villa dei Misteri** **E**. This aristocratic villa outside the city walls is known for the brightly hued fresco cycle that decorates the triclinium walls, depicting the initiation ceremony of a young bride into the cult of Dionysus.

Via dell'Abbondanza

To explore the eastern end of town, head back to the Forum and the **Via dell'Abbondanza** **F**. This street, lined with shops and taverns and cut through with cart tracks, would have been one of the town's busiest thoroughfares.

East of the Forum

On the left, the **Terme Stabiane** **G** were the city's largest baths, with separate sections for men and women, each with its own changing rooms. The Vicolo del Lupanare leads from here to the **Lupanare** **H**, one of 24 brothels in the city. Opposite the baths, on the right, Via dei Teitri leads to two amphitheatres: the **Teatro Grande** **I** and **Teatro Piccolo**, where plays were performed and concerts and poetry readings given; the former is still the venue for performances and events from June to September.

Vesuvius's eruptions

Following the catastrophic eruption, the plume of black smoke became a familiar sight on the skyline. Since its most recent eruption in 1944, however, when the cone collapsed into the crater, the volcano has been dormant, though fumaroles indicate a certain amount of activity. Today, its every movement is monitored by the Osservatorio Vesuviano (www.ov.ingv.it/ov), which has been recording data here since 1841 and celebrated the 175th anniversary of its foundation in 2016. You can climb to the rim safe in the knowledge that its expert vulcanologists are keeping a very close eye on things.

Anfiteatro and Palestra

At the end of Via dell'Abbondanza is the main **Anfiteatro** **J**. This colossal arena could seat fifteen thousand spectators and was reserved for gladiatorial combat; the colonnaded **Palestra** next door was the gladiatorial training ground. If you've brought a picnic, this is the perfect place – you can sit on the terraces and imagine Nero giving the thumbs-down from his imperial box below. Alternatively, retrace your steps to the Forum and have a picnic lunch in the designated area alongside the **Chora Café**, see **1**, behind the Temple of Jupiter.

A volcano victim

Pompeiian statue

Vesuvius

Take the train to the Ercolano Scavi station, which is the stop for both Vesuvius and Herculaneum. A visit to **Vesuvius ②** (www.parco nazionaledelvesuvio.it; Vesuvio; closed in bad weather), the only active volcano on the European mainland, makes a rewarding trip.

Climbing the crater

Vesuvio Express services (www.vesuvio express.it) run from Ercolano Scavi station to Vesuvius every 30–40 minutes. The minibus winds its way up the fertile slopes to the summit, where the landscape becomes dark and barren, stopping 1km (0.5 mile) from the top at a car park, from where it's

a 30-minute walk to the rim of the crater. The climb is not too extreme, but the winding lava-scree path is slippery, so take care. You can peer into the 200m- (650ft-) deep crater, but you can only go inside it on a guided walk.

Meet your minibus at the allotted time, and head back down to Ercolano Scavi station.

Herculaneum

You may have reached saturation point by now, but a visit to **Herculaneum ③** (https://ercolano.beniculturali.it) will prove highly rewarding. While most of Pompeii's buildings collapsed under the heavy downpour of rock and ash, in Herculaneum the upper floors of many of the houses withstood the force of the avalanche, and the dense coating of petrified mud encased and perfectly preserved their contents. It's a 10-minute walk downhill from the station, through the soulless modern town to the site; refuel at **La Fornacella**, see ②, before you explore the ruins.

Cardo III and IV

Walk from the entrance along Cardo III to the **Casa del Tramezzo di Legno ④** (House of the Wooden

Empty street in Herculaneum

Partition), so called because of the wooden screen separating the atrium from the *tablinum* (small office).

On the parallel Cardo IV, the **Casa a Graticcio** B (the Trellis House) is a humble two-storey dwelling with a balcony. North up the same street, the **Casa di Nettuno e Anfitrite** features a mosaic of Neptune; the next-door **Casa del Bel Cortile** C (House of the Beautiful Courtyard) holds three of the 300 skeletons unearthed by archaeologists in 1980 – a mother, father and child huddling together for comfort. At the other end of Cardo IV, seek out the **Casa dell'Atrio a Mosaico** D, an aristocratic residence with a geometric black-and-white mosaic on the atrium floor.

Cardo V

Cardo V holds the grandest house of all, the **Casa dei Cervi** E (House of the Deer), named after the sculptures found in the garden. Beyond here is a scenic terrace that would have overlooked the sea. South of here, the **Terme Suburbane** F (baths) are one of Herculaneum's best-preserved sites, complete with an intact Roman door – the only one on the site not charred by fire. On the site's eastern edge, the large **Palestra** (gymnasium complex) is where public games were held.

Villa dei Papiri

Recent excavations have concentrated on the **Villa dei Papiri** G, 150 metres

---

Food and Drink

➊ Chora Café
Pompeii Scavi;
www.chorapompeii.com; €
Pompeii's only place to eat is
a café/fast-food/restaurant
combo of indifferent quality
that gets fiendishly packed.

➋ La Fornacella
Via IV Novembre 90–92, Ercolano;
tel: 081-777 4861;
www.lafornacella.it; €
This well-located bar-restaurant,
100 metres from the station on the
road to Herculaneum, is ideal for
a snack or a quick meal and does
excellent slow-risen pizzas).

---

west of the exit, named after the 200 carbonised papyrus scrolls found here. Though closed at the time of writing, its many artworks and artefacts, including the Dancers of Herculaneum, can be seen in the Archaeological Museum.

Museo Archeologico Virtuale (MAV)

Near the entrance to Herculaneum at Via IV Novembre 44, the sleek **MAV** (www.museomav.it;) takes you on a virtual-reality journey through various Roman ruins, such as the Forum at Pompeii – an all-round sensory experience.

Wall mosaics of Venus and Neptune

TOUR 7
The Sorrentine Peninsula

A day and a night in the lively resort town of Sorrento, followed by a leisurely drive exploring the rugged Sorrentine Peninsula that divides the Bay of Naples from the Bay of Salerno.

DISTANCE: 23km (14.25 miles) on foot; 25km (15.5 miles) by car
TIME: Two days
START: Sorrento
END: Sant'Agata sui due Golfi
POINTS TO NOTE: Sorrento is easily reached from the Naples airport by Curreri coach (www.curreriviaggi. it), and by train from Naples on the Circumvesuviana line, but it's most fun to arrive by boat (from Naples' Beverello port). To explore the peninsula, you will need to either hire a car or a car with driver (www.benvenutolimos.com). SITA buses run to Amalfi and Positano from Sorrento.

The hook of land jutting from the southern end of the Bay of Naples is known as the Sorrentine Peninsula and forms part of the Monti Lattari range. Apart from Sorrento and a smattering of resort towns and hilltop villages, there is very little development, largely thanks to the inhospitable terrain in these parts. The craggy slopes are crisscrossed with ancient pathways and mule tracks that thread through olive and lemon groves into the hills and down to the sea.

Sorrento

Travellers have been falling for the charms of **Sorrento** ❶ since ancient times: it was founded by the Greeks (the grid of streets in the old town is their legacy) and adopted by rich Romans who built luxurious villas here. It was rediscovered as a summer retreat in the eighteenth century, when the ongoing excavations of Pompeii made it an obligatory stop on the Grand Tour. Scores of distinguished visitors stopped off to pay a visit to the genteel resort, from Byron and Sir Walter Scott to Wagner, Henry James, Goethe and Ibsen. These days it's a lively resort town occupying a low-key middle ground between gritty Naples and the chichi resorts along the coast. Despite its lack of a decent beach, it's a good option for families, and has long been a favourite with British tourists.

Sorrento harbour

Despite the crowds and tourist trappings, an air of elegance and romance prevails, and Sorrento's bustling, small-town street life makes it a rewarding place for an overnight stay.

The harbour

The most memorable way to arrive in Sorrento is by boat from Naples. Sorrento's harbour, Marina Piccola, huddles at the bottom of the long cliff on which the town is perched. Either walk south along Via Marina Piccola, then take the long flight of steps up to town, or hop on a bus from the harbour (buy your ticket from the information kiosk beforehand) up to Piazza Tasso. Most major hotels are within walking distance, but if you have luggage there are buses and taxis on the square.

Piazza Tasso

Sorrento's compact, walkable centre can easily be explored in half a day. Start at **Piazza Tasso** Ⓐ, the town's hub, flanked by bars and cafés, and busy day and night. Head west along busy, boutique-lined **Corso Italia**, stopping at **Primavera**, see ❶, the cream of the town's many *gelaterias*.

The Old Town

Continue west until you reach the **Duomo** Ⓑ. Sorrento's cathedral is unremarkable in itself, but the choir stalls show the local art of marquetry *(intarsia)* at its intricate best. Don't miss the lovely *presepe* to the left of the entrance, in which the news of Christ's birth interrupts the locals as they sit down to a fish dinner.

Beyond the Duomo, cross the road and venture into the old town. Running parallel to Corso Italia, the skinny **Via San Cesareo** Ⓒ is a riot of souvenir shops, hawking *limoncello* and a host of lemon-themed knick-knacks. On the corner of Via Giuliani is the **Sedile Dominova** Ⓓ, a beautiful sixteenth-century loggia, with a domed trompe l'œil cupola, that was the summer meeting place for Sorrentine aristocrats.

Villa Comunale

Walk downhill from here along Via Giuliani, turning right on to Via Vittorio Veneto, then left for the **Villa Comunale** Ⓔ, a shady park at the cliff's edge with wonderful views over the bay. At the edge of the park stands the Baroque church of **San Francesco** Ⓕ its bell tower topped with an onion dome. The medieval cloister makes a stunning venue for the classical and jazz concerts of the **Sorrento Festival**.

The beach

From the Villa Comunale, take the steps down to the beach platforms of **Marina Piccola** Ⓖ. Sorrento is not known for its beaches, but if your hotel doesn't have a pool, the

Sedile Dominova

Duomo artwork

handful of public *stabilimenti* (Apr–early Octare well placed for soaking up the sun. You'll pay a daily fee for entrance and a sun lounger, and most have a snack bar on site.

Basilica di Sant'Antonino

Back at San Francesco, take the road bearing left, which opens out on to Piazza Sant'Antonino, planted with shady palms and orange trees. Overlooking the square, the **Basilica di Sant'Antonino** has an ornate Baroque interior, from its chandeliers to its gold ceiling panels. Look out for the ex-votos from shipwrecked sailors: the local Saint Antoninus apparently rescued a child after it had been swallowed by a whale, and as

such is the protector of those at sea. Outside the church, turn sharp right to reach the exceptional **Il Buco**, tucked into the church's stone vaults.

Museo Correale di Terranova

Back on the piazza, turn left to rejoin Piazza Tasso, left along Corso Italia and left again at the canary-yellow church into Via Correale. A five-minute stroll takes you to the **Museo Correale di Terranova** (Via Correale 48; www.museocorreale.it). The museum gets its name from brothers and art connoisseurs Alfredo and Pompeo Correale, counts of Terranova, who bequeathed their family's art collection to the city in 1924. Paintings by Neapolitan greats

Villa Comunale offers great views

Golfo di Napoli

Via Califano

GIARDINO
SORRENTINO

**Museo Correale
di Terranova** ❶

Via Rota

Via Correale

Via B. Canasso

Piazza
Lauro

Corso Italia

Piazza
Curtis
Stazione
Circumvesuviana

Via degli Aranci

such as Luca Giordano and Giovanni Lanfranco, silverware, bronzes, *presepe* figurines, and a whole floor dedicated to porcelain and majolica make up the varied collection.

Marina Grande

Join the post-*passeggiata* throngs for an *aperitivo* in Piazza Tasso; buzzy **Fauno Bar**, see ❷, is the best place to kick off your evening. From here it's a 20-minute walk down to **Marina Grande** ❶. Make your way to Piazza della Vittoria and follow Via Marina Grande down to the harbour, confusingly called Marina Grande, the 'Big Port', as opposed to Marina Piccola, or 'Little Port': it is in fact the smaller and more down-

at-heel of the two, but all the more charming for it. The tiny church of Sant'Anna in the harbour, with an array of ex-votos, is sometimes atmospherically candlelit at night.

The harbour is one of the most authentic corners of Sorrento. In the evening, the restaurants that hog the waterfront twinkle invitingly; for atmosphere, **Da Emilia**, see ❸, is hard to beat.

The Peninsula

Spend your second day exploring the Sorrento Peninsula. Exit Sorrento on Via Capo, which begins at the eastern end of Corso Italia. At the first fork turn right and follow the signs to Massa. The first stop is the small village of **Capo di Sorrento** ❷, where you can take the steep Roman road down towards the sea. It's a 10-minute walk past olive trees and oleander bushes to the ruins of the first-century **Villa di Pollio Felice**, spread across a precipice. A wooden walkway skirts the rocky coast to the Bagni della Regina Giovanna, a rocky beach with crystal-clear water.

Punta Campanella

The next settlement is **Massa Lubrense** ❸, actually seventeen hamlets divided by olive groves. Make a pitstop in the square, admire the sixteenth-century Neapolitan paintings inside the church, and gaze at the view from the belvedere before moving on

The beach   Marina Grande

to **Termini** ❹, the departure point of one of the loveliest walks on the peninsula. Park outside the yellow church and follow the signs to the Punto Panoramico to reach **Punta Campanella** ❺. The road soon gives way to a footpath that descends slowly through terraced lemon and olive groves, past a Saracen watchtower, to the tip of the peninsula. The point is thought to be named after the warning bell (*campanella*) that was rung when Turkish pirates were sighted. The views from here are breathtaking and Capri is so close you could almost reach out and touch it. Allow for about two hours in total.

Bay of Ieranto

The coast from here to Positano is wild and rugged. The limestone cliffs sliced with deep ravines plunge into hidden coves that can only be reached by boat. It's largely inaccessible by car but a walker's paradise. The villages are linked by a series of footpaths that take you through citrus groves, chestnut and oak copses, and uninhabited areas blanketed in thick Mediterranean vegetation; see www.giovis.com for routes.

Marina del Cantone is the only bay with a road link. On the winding road down to the bay is the sleepy village of **Nerano** ❻. From its piazza you can make the 45-minute walk along the cliffs to the **Marina di Ieranto** ❼, where you'll be rewarded with a spectacular beach.

Marina del Cantone

The road ends at **Marina del Cantone** ❽. It has a small, pebbly beach, but the real draw is its seafood restaurants, including the **Taverna del Capitano** (see page 101).

Sweeping view of the coast

Food and Drink

① Primavera
Corso Italia 142;
www.primaverasorrento.it; €
This crowded *gelateria* is plastered with photos of celebrities enjoying the excellent ice cream made here. The *agrumeto Sorrentino* and *crema di limone* flavours, made with local lemons, are delicious.

② Fauno Bar
Piazza Tasso 13/15; www.faunobar.it; €
This venerable old-timer has a real buzz about it in the evening,

when white-jacketed waiters weave between the tables, carrying trays of *aperitivi*. An outdoor table here is pricier than elsewhere but worth it for the prime location.

③ Da Emilia
Via Marina Grande 62;
tel: 081-807 2720; daily 12.15–3pm, 6–10pm; www.daemilia.it; €€
This waterfront trattoria has been run by the same family since 1947, and its friendly, homely atmosphere ensures that it's always packed. Impeccably cooked, tasty food.

Sant'Agata sui due Golfi

The scenic road up to the town of **Sant'Agata sui due Golfi ❾** is lined with olive groves, as well as myrtle, gorse and strawberry trees; even wild orchids thrive in this fertile soil. Sant'Agata is a nondescript town that has been put on the map thanks to one of Italy's most famous restaurants – gourmets travel for miles to sample the culinary masterpieces served up at **Don Alfonso 1890** (see page 100). The church on the same square has a beautiful altar inlaid with mother-of-pearl and lapis lazuli. Follow the signs 1km (0.5 mile) uphill to the **Il Deserto** convent (tel: 081-878 0199; call in advance to arrange access). The building looks more like a high-security prison than a convent, but

the views from the roof terrace are breathtaking. This is the only place along the coast from which you can see both the Gulf of Naples and the Gulf of Salerno, hence the name (*due golfi*: two gulfs). The road out of Sant'Agata joins the SS163; turn left to return to Sorrento or right to continue to Positano.

Monte Faito

In summer, visit Monte Faito for its lovely walks, cooling breezes and spectacular views. The *funivia* (cable car) is accessed from the Castellammare di Stabia stop on the Circumvesuviana line (Apr–Oct; every 20–30 mins). Bring a picnic, as there are no places to buy provisions beyond the funicular bars.

Steps down to the beach

WALK 8
Positano

The coast's most photogenic town offers welcome respite from a sights-packed itinerary. It's the perfect place to spend a few hours lazing on the beach, pottering around the shops and soaking up the atmosphere.

DISTANCE: 2km (1.25 miles)
TIME: Half a day
START: Upper town
END: Fornillo Beach
POINTS TO NOTE: There is a good bus service (SITA) between Sorrento, Positano (50 mins) and Amalfi (1hr 40min). In summer, ferries usually run to Positano from Sorrento and Naples, as well as from Ischia and Capri, so this route could be combined with routes 10 and 11, although the more traditional pairing would be with the Amalfi Coast drive (route 9). The best source of transport information (with booking links) is www.positano.com.

With its near-vertical jumble of pastel-coloured houses clinging to cliffs that drop to a black-sand bay lined with rows of parasols, **Positano** is undeniably easy on the eye. Its charms have secured its place as the coast's most chichi resort, but stroll along the beach and you'll see that it's not entirely geared towards high-end tourism:

among the serried ranks of pricey sun loungers, local families still spread out their towels and tuck into picnics.

The town became fashionable after World War II. 'Positano bites deep,' wrote a spellbound John Steinbeck. 'It is a dream that isn't quite real when you are there and becomes beckoningly real after you have gone.' Positano's quiet romance disappeared with the tourists that followed in Steinbeck's wake, though some of its old magic remains, especially after dark, when the town is lit up with fairy lights and restaurant tables spill out on to the stepped streets.

Upper town

SITA services drop off at the Sponda stop, from where it's a short stroll along **Via Cristoforo Colombo** ❶ to the lower town. If you're driving, leave your car in one of the car parks at the top end of town. Wend your way downhill.

Lower town

Steeply sloping **Via dei Mulini** ❷ heads down towards the sea; stop

Delightful Positano

for a pastry at **La Zagara**, see ❶, before exploring the town. A little further down the street, peek into the beautiful flower-filled courtyard of **Palazzo Murat** on the left, once the residence of Joachim Murat, French king of Naples in the eighteenth century and husband to Napoleon's sister Caroline; it's now one of Positano's loveliest hotels (see page 93). Along this stretch and off the souk-like side streets are numerous boutiques, specialising in womenswear, leather sandals and swimwear.

Santa Maria Assunta

Via dei Mulini's overhead trellis hung with pink bougainvillea makes this a stunning approach to **Santa Maria Assunta** ❸ (Piazza Flavio Gioia). The church's Moorish green-and-yellow-tiled dome graces every postcard you'll see of Positano. Inside

Boat trips

If there's one place on the Amalfi Coast that deserves to be seen from the sea, it's Positano. Several companies set up shop on the beaches in summer, offering day trips to Capri, along the Amalfi Coast, and to the **Grotta dello Smeraldo** (Emerald Grotto) – a shadowy grotto bathed in a shimmering emerald-green light – as well as sunset cruises to the Li Galli islands (although as this is private land, you can't go ashore). Alternatively, rent your own boat with skipper. Details at www.positano.com.

is the prized thirteenth-century Black Madonna icon, which is thought to hold the origins of the town's name – the story goes that when pirates tried to steal the figure, a booming command from Heaven to put it back 'posa, posa' ('put it down' in Latin) was supposedly heard.

Spiaggia Grande

Take the steps from the piazza down to the **Spiaggia Grande ❹**, the town's main beach and one of Positano's major draws – although the beach is shingly, the water is clean, and the beach is broad and backed by bars and restaurants. It can be very crowded in summer; and sun lounger hire is steep. There is a small *spiaggia libera* ('free beach'), a sun lounger-free patch that's popular with families, but this is inevitably towel-to-towel in high season.

Via Positanesi d'America

Take **Via Positanesi d'America ❺**, the spectacular seafront path that begins by the harbour and links the town's two beaches. The path winds along the bottom of the cliff, passing the Torre Trasita, one of the coast's many watchtowers, and **Lo Guarracino**, see ❷. The path also offers glorious views of the cluster of islets called **Li Galli**; thanks to its resemblance to a curvaceous woman floating in an azure sea, locals have nicknamed it Brigitte Bardot – appropriate given it is the place where Ulysses is thought to have been tempted by the seductive song of the sirens.

Food and Drink

❶ La Zagara

Via dei Mulini 4; www.lazagara.com; €
This local institution, named after the orange trees (zagara means orange blossom) that grow on its interior terrace, has a tempting array of pastries; try the Zagara, a chocolate sponge cake made with tangerine syrup. In the later part of the evening La Zagara turns into a lively piano-bar.

❷ Lo Guarracino

Via Positanesi d'America 12;
www.loguarracinopositano.it; €€
This trattoria's scenic terrace, surrounded by olive and prickly pear trees, is what makes it special. Tasty pizzas and fish dishes are on the menu, as well as simple meat *secondi* such as veal escalope in lemon sauce. Booking is essential on summer evenings.

Spiaggia Fornillo

At the end of the path is **Spiaggia Fornillo ❻**, the beach named after the bakers' ovens used here in Roman times. It's more down-to-earth than the Spiaggia Grande, with a few low-key beach bars and restaurants. The Fornillo district clings to the hillside behind, its peaceful lanes a world away from the glitz of central Positano.

Exploring Positano

TOUR 9
Amalfi and Ravello

One of the world's most iconic drives, the serpentine Amalfi Coast road is breathtaking and nerve-jangling in equal measure. The tour takes in two of the coast's most picturesque towns, Amalfi and Ravello, and an optional hike in the beautiful Lattari mountains.

DISTANCE: 12km (7.5 miles) on foot, or 22km (13.5 miles) including the Sentiero degli Dei, plus 3.5km (2 miles) by car or public transport
TIME: Two days
START: Amalfi
END: Montepertuso
POINTS TO NOTE: The corniche coast road (SS163) requires nerves of steel – buses rocket round the bends with nonchalant ease, but drivers would be unwise to try the same. Traffic can be appalling in summer, so set out early. If you'd rather leave the driving to the locals, take the regular SITA bus service to Amalfi from Sorrento railway station (1hr 30 mins). Queue early for a window seat (on the right going out). There are frequent buses from Amalfi to Ravello (25 mins). In summer, boats run between Sorrento, Capri and the Amalfi Coast resorts.

The drive along the Costiera Amalfitana is one heart-stopping journey you won't forget. The 50km (31-mile) ribbon of road snakes its way between Sant'Agata sui due Golfi and Salerno, with vertiginous views of the sea below and the mountains above.

Amalfi

Having passed Positano (see route 8), the road winds its way round plunging valleys and soaring cliffs that drop almost sheer into the sea. The first major stop is cheerful **Amalfi ❶**. At the height of its power in the eleventh century, the Maritime Republic of Amalfi rivalled the northern ports of Pisa, Genoa and Venice. Amalfitan merchants traded with Byzantium, Asia Minor and Africa, making it the most important port in southern Italy.

Nestling in a ravine, its tightly packed houses seem to tumble down to the tiny port below. Cars and buses park outside the city wall on Piazza Flavio Gioia.

Duomo and town centre

Pass through the arch into Piazza Duomo, dominated by the **Duomo ❹**, a striking example of Arab-Norman

Amalfi rooftops

architecture. A steep flight of steps leads to the Moorish archways and facade inlaid with geometric mosaics – a nineteenth-century reconstruction of the original. The bell tower (1276) and bronze doors, cast in Constantinople in the eleventh century, are from the original structure, as is the **Chiostro del Paradiso** (1266). This atmospheric cloister with Arabesque arches was the cemetery of Amalfitan nobles. In the crypt lies part of the skull of St Andrew, patron saint of Amalfi.

Back on Piazza Duomo, stop for a sweet treat you may remember for the rest of your life at historic **Pansa**, see ①. The square is awash with day-trippers, but off the main drag you'll soon lose yourself in the narrow, whitewashed side streets and covered alleyways. Among the countless souvenir shops is the odd gem, such as **Antichi Sapori d'Amalfi** (Supportico Ferrari 4; www. antichisaporidamalfi.it), a great place for souvenirs like fruity liqueurs.

Walk back towards Piazza Flavio Gioia and to the **Antico Arsenale della Repubblica** ❸ (Largo Cesareo Console 3; www.arsenalediamalfi.it), a collection of old shipyards converted into an exciting new exhibition space. It's also the site of the **Museo della Bussola e del Ducato Marinaro di Amalfi**, which is dedicated to Amalfi's heyday as a maritime republic and the history of the compass, which, according to local folklore, was invented by the Amalfitano Flavio Gioia in 1302. It

houses local memorabilia and costumes from the town's historic regatta, the Festa delle Antiche Repubbliche Marinare, held annually in late May or June. Every four years, the Regatta of the Ancient Maritime Republics – Amalfi, Pisa, Venice and Genoa – comes to town, with a spectacular race ending in the harbour (last held in 2022). If you are hungry, stop at **Cuoppo d'Amalfi**, see ②, for amazing fried fish to take away or eat on a bench outside.

Duomo statuary

Paper Museum

Further north up the main **Via Pietro Capuano** , the tourist shops peter out, and once you reach Via delle Cartiere, Amalfi

takes on an entirely different persona, more villagey and with the odd reminder of the industry that was once the town's big earner: sixty paper mills once operated here. The **Museo della Carta** (Paper Museum; Via delle Cartiere 23; www.museodellacarta.it), gives demonstrations in the thirteenth-century paper mill downstairs.

Valle dei Mulini

Opposite the museum, the road that leads round to the right, then the steps up to the left lead to the **Valle dei Mulini** ('Valley of the Mills'), a wooded valley of wild flowers and waterfalls, which ends in terraced lemon groves: a walk of around an hour and a half.

Atrani

From Amalfi's waterfront, it's a 15-minute stroll east to **Atrani** , a workaday place with some good, authentic trattorias. Walk past the Saracen tower (now the restaurant of the Hotel Luna Convento, where Ibsen wrote *A Doll's House*) and around the headland to reach the beach. It has

the same silvery sand as in Amalfi, but makes a much more peaceful place to laze in the sun. **Le Arcate**, see , right by the beach, is a lovely spot for lunch, after which you could explore Atrani's whitewashed alleyways.

Ravello

Back on the coast road, take the left turn to Ravello, just past Atrani. The road climbs steeply for a few kilometres until the picture-perfect town comes into view, spilling down the hillside. Between the eleventh and thirteenth centuries, wealthy merchants imported the Moorish artefacts and architectural styles that remain one of the town's glories.

Of the three main resorts along the coast, **Ravello** is the more refined and tranquil. Alternatively, buses usually run back down to Amalfi quite late, so you could have dinner here before heading back down; ask at the tourist office for schedules (Via Roma 18bis; www.ravello.com or www.sitasudtrasporti.com).

Duomo interior

Duomo façade and bell tower

Ravello festival

Every year, from July to September, sleepy Ravello adjusts to a huge increase in visitor numbers as it hosts the world-renowned Ravello Festival (www.ravellofestival.com), a series of open-air concerts by prestigious performers. A concert under the stars in such atmospheric locations as Villas Rufolo and Cimbrone is a spine-tingling experience not to be missed by classical music fans. An added attraction is the space-age auditorium, designed by Brazilian architect Oscar Niemeyer. Ten years in the making, it offers both impressive acoustics and staggering views.

The Duomo

The town is closed to traffic, so park on the outskirts and walk in. The bus from Amalfi stops outside a tunnel that leads straight to the main Piazza del Duomo, the archetypal small-town Italian square, with a handful of cafés and shops arranged around a medieval cathedral. The **Duomo** is dedicated to St Pantaleone and holds two splendid Byzantine pulpits. The attached museum houses sculptures, bronze artefacts and religious art.

Villa Rufolo and Villa Cimbrone

The real reason for coming to Ravello is its two lovely villas – or more accurately, their gardens. **Villa Rufolo** ❹

(www.villarufolo.it), in the shadow of the cathedral, was built in the Moorish style by the Rufolo dynasty, the richest family in medieval Ravello. Here, Wagner found inspiration for the magic garden in *Parsifal*, his last opera, in 1880. In summer, the gardens host the prestigious Ravello Festival.

The town's other landmark is the **Villa Cimbrone** (www.villacimbrone. com), a pleasant 15-minute walk from the square. The villa was designed in the early twentieth century by the eccentric Lord Grimthorpe, best known for designing the clock on London's Houses of Parliament. Today it's a luxury hotel, but you can still visit the terraced gardens and the magnificent balcony hanging 300m (980ft) above sea level.

Path of the Gods

If you have a day to spare, consider venturing out on one of the many walking trails that cut through the Monti Lattari. One of the best is the **Sentiero degli Dei** ❺ – the Path of the Gods, between the mountain villages of Bomerano, west of Amalfi, and Nocelle, east of Positano.

Catch the earliest bus you can from Amalfi to Bomerano; the trail markings begin at the main square. It's a gentle three-hour walk through vineyards, lemon and cypress groves, and wild Mediterranean *macchia* (scrub) along a path suspended between sea and sky. The views are awe-inspiring. The

Al fresco dining in Ravello

Food and Drink

1 Pansa

Piazza Duomo 40, Amalfi;
www.pasticceriapansa.it; €
This historic *pasticceria* is an elegant
spot for a coffee and pastry, lined
with vintage wood cabinets and
age-spotted mirrors. For breakfast
go for a sfogliatelle, and for an
afternoon treat e sure to try one of
Pansa's citrus specialities: *delizia al
limone*, stuffed with lemon cream
and flavoured with *limoncello*, or
chocolate-coated candied orange peel.

2 Cuoppo d'Amalfi

Via Supportico dei Ferrari 10,
Amalfi off Piazza dei Dogi; €
A cuoppo is Neapolitan dialect for a
cone of paper, filled with freshly deep-
fried fish and seafood. It is traditional
seaside streetfood, to eat as you
wander along. This place is unmissable,
its calamari, shrimps and anchovies
deep-fried to perfection in cardboard
cones, to be eaten on the bench outside.
It may well be the best fish of your
entire holiday – the batter is made of
rice flour, so is gluten free to boot.

3 Le Arcate

Largo Cav. Orlando Buonocore, Atrani;
www.learcate.net; €€
Tucked into a corner of Atrani's
harbour, Le Arcate's waterfront tables
enjoy a location that would be hard to
beat. The simple menu is strong on
fish – grilled catch of the day with a
simple salad makes a delicious lunch
– and there are pizzas in the evening.

4 Trattoria Santa Croce

Via Nocelle 19, Nocelle; www.ristorante
santacrocepositano.com; €€
Reward yourself after the Sentiero
degli Dei with lunch at this tranquil
restaurant. The antipasti plate makes
a generous starter to share, and the
mixed fried fish – the house speciality
– is superb. Book a window table to
make the most of the stunning views.

walk ends at Nocelle, where the sky-
high **Trattoria Santa Croce**, see 4,
serves wonderful home-cooking.

Montepertuso

If you're tired, take the bus from
Nocelle to Positano via **Montepertuso**
6. Or walk down (see walk 8), from
where there are buses to Amalfi.

On the descent to Montepertuso,
look out for the huge hole that pierces
a vast rock on the mountainside. Local
legend has it the hole was created by the
Virgin Mary when the Devil challenged
her to a contest: whoever pierced
the rock would own the land. When
Mary touched the rock, it crumbled,
leaving a hole that swallowed him up.

The Sentiero degli Dei

Cheerful ceramics in Ravello

TOUR 10
Capri

An overnight stay on one of the Mediterranean's most dazzling islands, taking in its two towns – glitzy Capri and lofty Anacapri – and walking its beautiful coastline, with panoramic views at every turn.

DISTANCE: 8.5km (5.25 miles) on foot plus 7.5km (4.5 miles) by public transport
TIME: Two days
START: The Piazzetta
END: Grotta Azzurra
POINTS TO NOTE: Hydrofoils and ferries to Capri depart regularly from Naples and Sorrento, and less regularly and seasonally from Amalfi. Buy your return ticket early if you're not staying the night, as the later boats fill up quickly. Note that the Blue Grotto is closed if the sea is rough. Capri is hilly, so for the walks you'll need sturdy shoes, but anyone reasonably fit will find they can walk just about everywhere. If not, there is a decent bus service, and several places renting out scooters. Alternatively, get around on two wheels – there are several places renting out scooters (www.capri.com). The island's open-top taxis are plentiful but pricey.

With its soaring cliffs, emerald waters, lush vegetation and whitewashed towns, Capri is a capsule of Mediterranean beauty. The Emperor Augustus fell in love with the island when he arrived here in 29 BC and traded the fertile island of Ischia for this rocky paradise that had belonged to Naples. His adopted son Tiberius ruled the Roman Empire from here until his death. Capri's charms have been exalted by playwrights, poets and novelists through the ages, but these days, it is the island's jet-set glamour that is a magnet to visitors.

Around Capri Town

Boats arrive at **Marina Grande**. Before catching the funicular up to **Capri Town ❶**, buy tickets at the kiosk.

You emerge from the funicular on Piazza Umberto I. Known as the **Piazzetta**, this diminutive square, overlooked by the church of **Santo Stefano**, is the departure point for many lovely walks; the best is the 45-minute stroll up to Villa Jovis, the ancient ruins of Tiberius's palace on the eastern tip of the island. Exit the square on Via Le Botteghe in the far right-hand corner and follow the well-marked route through the whitewashed streets, past walled

Villa Jovis

gardens and olive groves. The climb is steep at points, but worth the effort for the views over the Bay of Naples.

Villa Jovis and the Arco Naturale

Villa Jovis ❷ (www.coopculture.it) was the grandest of twelve palaces that the emperor Tiberius had built on Capri. He ruled the Roman Empire from here for ten years, between wild orgies and nights of debauchery. On the highest point is the **Salto di Tiberio** (Tiberius's Leap), from where the emperor hurled his enemies and unsatisfactory lovers. Nowadays it's an evocatively overgrown ruin.

On the way back down, when you reach the crossroads at the bottom of Via Tiberio, turn left into Via Matermánia and follow signs to the **Arco Naturale**

❸, a huge outcrop of limestone rock that has been eroded by the sea into a natural arch. Backtrack up the winding path to **Le Grottelle**, see ❶.

Belvedere di Tragara

From the restaurant, steps lead down to a coastal footpath and the **Grotta di Matermánia ❹**, a cave converted into a *nymphaeum* (fountain dedicated to water nymphs) by the Ancient Romans. Further along, the strange red villa balanced on the edge of a low-lying promontory to your left belonged to the writer Curzio Malaparte (1898–1957). The path ends at the terrace of the **Belvedere di Tragara ❺**, with captivating views of the **Faraglioni**, a trio of rocks that are the habitat of the rare blue lizard.

The Arco Naturale

The Belvedere di Tragara

Sentiero dei Fortini

To avoid the crowds, catch a bus from Anacapri to Punta Carena (take a bus signed 'Faro' from Via de Tommaso), one of the wildest corners of the island and the departure point for a stunning walk. The **Sentiero dei Fortini** hugs the west coast from the lighthouse at Punta Carena to the Punta dell'Arcera near the Blue Grotto, passing three ruined fortresses along the way. Mostly easy going, it takes about three hours each way. There are lots of places to swim en route, but returning ashore is not always easy, except at Punta Carena.

Certosa di San Giacomo

It's a short walk back to the centre along Via Tragara and Via Camerelle, where you can browse in designer stores. At the top of Via Camerelle, turn left after the historic Hotel Quisisana into Via Serena, which leads to the **Certosa di San Giacomo** ❻. This medieval charterhouse is now home to a small museum, containing statues found in the Blue Grotto and paintings by the German Symbolist Karl Wilhelm Diefenbach.

Giardini di Augusto

Come out of the monastery and take the left-hand Via Matteotti at the junction with Via Serena for the **Giardini di Augusto** ❼ (www.coopculture. it and www.capriculturaeturismo. it), which are terraced gardens offering more dazzling views.

At sunset, the Piazzetta regains its composure. Emptied of day-trippers, the little square turns into an outdoor salon as the *beau monde* emerges from the hotels for a night out. Join them for a cocktail; Piccolo Bar is the oldest and least showy of the quartet of bars. For dinner, the terrace at **Pulalli** (see page 104) can't be beaten.

Around Anacapri

Day two is spent exploring Anacapri and the west coast. Capri's second town is more rustic than its worldly rival, with a Moorish influence visible in its cubic whitewashed houses. Buses from Via Roma in Capri town run to **Piazza Vittoria**, which is crammed with souvenir shops.

In the piazza, walk up the steps and turn left for **Villa San Michele** ❽ (34 Viale Axel Munthe; www.villa sanmichele.eu), built by the Swedish doctor Axel Munthe (1857–1949) on the ruins of one of Tiberius's villas. His book, *The Story of San Michele*, describing the building of his villa was an international bestseller. The house is now a museum with a display of ancient finds and eclectic furnishings, but the lush garden is the highlight, with its vine-swathed pergola framing jaw-dropping views. It makes a spectacular venue for concerts under the stars in the summer. Don't miss the Egyptian

Inside the Certosa di San Giacomo

Sphinx on the parapet of the chapel, on the garden's top level. **Café Casa Oliv**, see ❷, on the roof terrace is a delightful place for lunch or a glass of wine.

Monte Solaro
In the corner of Piazza Vittoria, a chair-lift whisks you up to the summit of **Monte Solaro** ❾ (589m/1,932ft; www.capriseggiovia.it). The wonderful, peaceful ride over gardens, woods and vineyards takes just under quarter of an hour, and more spellbinding views and a bar welcome you at the top.

Church of San Michele
Leading off Piazza Vittoria, Via Orlandi takes you to the Pompeiian-red **Casa Rossa** ❿ at No. 78 (www.museocasa rossa.it) containing finds from the Blue Grotto. Continue on Via Orlandi, turning right on to Piazza San Nicola for the church of **San Michele** ⓫, which is renowned for its majolica floor, depicting the expulsion from Paradise.

Grotta Azzurra
If you didn't succumb to one of the boat trips offered at Marina Grande, catch a bus to the **Grotta Azzurra** ⓬ Capri's biggest tourist attraction. Descend the steps to the cave entrance and join the queue for the boatmen who row endless streams of tourists around the marine cavern. The best time to visit is between 11am and 1pm, when the cave walls are bathed in an intense aquamarine light, while

Food and Drink

❶ Le Grottelle
Via Arco Naturale 13; tel: 081-837 5719; €€€
Suspended above a verdant hillside overlooking the sea, this is an irresistible lunch spot, strong on fish dishes such as baked anchovies with local herbs. Booking is essential for the panoramic terrace.

❷ Café Casa Oliv
Villa San Michele, Viale Axel Munthe 34; www.villasanmichele.eu; €
Lovely place for a light lunch, coffee, sandwich or glass of wine, on the roof terrace of Villa San Michele. The views are wonderful, and in season tomatoes, lemons and herbs come from the villa's garden.

❸ Il Riccio
Via Gradola 4 ; www.jumeirah.com/en/dine/italy/il-riccio-restaurant; €€€
Gorgeous upmarket seafood restaurant right beside the grotto, located in the rather exclusive beach club setting of Capri Palace Jumeirah. The terrace (heated off-season) teetering above the sparkling sea is hard to beat. Smart casual dress.

the sandy bottom glows with silvery shadows. The restaurant **Il Riccio**, see ❸, is just steps from the grotto.

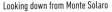
Looking down from Monte Solaro

Lush garden at Villa San Michele

TOUR 11
Ischia

This two-day tour of the lush 'emerald island' of Ischia does a loop of the island, taking in its bustling towns and stopping for a spot of pampering in its celebrated hot springs.

DISTANCE: 10km (6.25 miles) on foot plus 38km (23.5 miles) by car/bus

TIME: Two days

START: Ischia Porto

END: Ischia Ponte

POINTS TO NOTE: Hydrofoils and ferries depart from Naples, Sorrento and Pozzuoli to Ischia Porto, Casamicciola and Forio. Bus #CS from Ischia Porto cover the (anticlockwise) circular route described here about every 30 mins; the loop takes around two hours. Bus #CD follows the same route in a clockwise direction; single tickets and day passes are both available (www.ischiainsider.com). Most hotels close from mid-October to Easter; many will insist on half-board in summer but agree to bed and breakfast in low season. Ischia is an easy place to navigate. The best way to explore is by car or scooter - Balestrieri Rent A Car (Via Iasolino 35; www.autonoleggiobalestrieri.it) has both.

Ischia may not have the same rugged beauty as its neighbour, but it has great beaches and protected inland areas that are a haven for walkers. As well as yielding excellent wine, the volcanic terrain produces bubbling hot springs, prized for their therapeutic powers.

Ischia was first settled by Greek traders in the eighth century BC, followed by the Romans who flocked to its spas. But less than a century after Pompeii, Monte Epomeo erupted, destroying all life on the island. From the Middle Ages, the islanders lived in fear of marauding Saracens, who remained a threat for centuries. It wasn't until the nineteenth century and the advent of the Grand Tourists that Ischia regained its status as a prestigious spa resort.

Around Ischia Porto

Most boats from Naples stop at **Ischia Porto ❶**, a harbour whose natural boundaries once enclosed a volcanic crater lake. A string of fish restaurants lines the harbour.

The beach at Forio

This route follows the SS270 ring road in a westerly direction. **Casamícciola Terme ❷**, the first major town, has numerous spa hotels, but the best places are elsewhere.

Lacco Ameno

Carry on to **Lacco Ameno ❸**, site of the first Greek settlement. Just before the town beach, the SS270 veers inland, but continue along the seafront to admire the town's symbol, **Il Fungo**: a rock sculpted by erosion into a mushroom shape rising out of the sea. The road ends in a square

with a pink church dedicated to the island's patron saint, **Santa Restituta**. The **Area Archeologica** next door holds Greco-Roman remains.

Just off the square, a slope climbs to the eighteenth-century Villa Arbusto, home to the **Museo Archeologico di Pithecusae** (Corso Rizzoli 210; www.pithecusae.it) and more ancient treasures. The star exhibit is the seventh-century 'Nestor's Cup', described in the *Iliad* and bearing one of the oldest Greek inscriptions in existence, praising the wines of Ischia.

Giardini la Mortella

Taking the waters

According to legend, an exhausted Ulysses regained his strength after wallowing in Casamicciola's hot springs, and Ischia's 103 springs and 67 fumaroles still do an excellent job of soothing weary limbs. Head for Negombo for cutting-edge treatments, Giardini Poseidon Terme and Aphrodite Apollon (www.aphroditeapollon.it) for mud baths and the spa at the Albergo della Regina Isabella (see page 95) for a more intimate spa experience.

Negombo

The SS270 continues uphill, skirting **Monte Vico** (116m/381ft). This lofty promontory boasts the island's prettiest beach, the **Baia di San Montano**, and its most exclusive spa, **Negombo** 4 (Via San Montano 14; www.negombo.it), where fifteen pools, caves and baths are arranged in terraces dotted with sculptures.

La Mortella

Hidden among the signs at the next right-hand turning is one to **La Mortella** 5 (Via F. Calise 39; www.lamortella.org), the estate of English composer Sir William Walton (1902–83). It is famous for its gardens, planted with 1,200 species and cultivated over fifty years by Walton's widow, Lady Susana, until

her death in 2010. Concerts and Greek theatre performances are held here in spring, summer and autumn.

Around Forio

Past La Mortella, the road carries on to the Spiaggia San Francesco, a little stretch of beach, then rejoins the SS270 at lively **Forio** 6. Stroll into the historic centre along Corso Umberto and follow signs to the white church of **Madonna del Soccorso**, filled with offerings for the protection of fishermen and sailors. (see page 105).

The nearest decent beach is **Citara**, most of which has been colonised by the **Giardini Poseidon** 7 (www.giardiniposeidonterme.com). This spa has a more old-fashioned feel than Negombo, but its 21 pools and range of treatments make it popular.

For the chance to test some local wines stop by the **Pietratorcia Winery** 8, see 1.

Sant'Angelo

Come off the SS270 at Panza and follow signs to **Sant'Angelo** 9 on the southernmost tip of the island; park outside the town. Sant'Angelo is not the untouched fishing village it once was, but something of its old character remains in the narrow streets and stack of pastel and white houses.

East of the village is the **Terme Aphrodite Apollon** spa

Charming Forio

(www.aphroditeapollon.it); beyond is the **Spiaggia dei Maronti**, a long stretch of public beach that can be reached via a clifftop footpath or by water taxi from the port.

Monte Epomeo

Back inland, the road winds its way up into the mountainous heartland. At the village of Fontana, take the first left after the little square, signposted for **Monte Epomeo** ⑩, which will take you halfway up the extinct volcano of Monte Epomeo, Ischia's highest point at 787m (2,582ft). Park at the bar and make the 40-minute trek to the top. Magnificent, 360-degree views of the island await you. Reward yourself with a drink at **La Grotta da Fiore**, see ❷.

Ischia Ponte

The SS270 completes its circle at **Ischia Ponte** ⑪, where the hulking **Castello Aragonese** (www.castello aragoneseischia.com) lords it over the town. Park by the sea, then cross the Ponte Aragonese to the medieval castle.

The Greeks built the first fortress on this rocky islet in 474 BC. It was enlarged by subsequent rulers and, in 1441, Alfonso of Aragon strengthened the defences and added the bridge, enabling locals to take refuge within its walls during pirate attacks. By the eighteenth century, the island had thirteen churches and a thriving community, but in

1809, under French rule, it was bombarded by the British and all but destroyed. On July 26 each year, the Festa di Sant'Anna sees a spectacular sea-borne procession staging the 'burning of the Castello Aragonese', culminating in an extravagant firework display.

Take the lift to the top, where you can wander a network of paths that take you past the ruined shells of churches, taking in the heart-stopping views from the ancient defences. If you want to wake up to that same view, book a room at **Il Monastero** (see page 95).

The village has lots of lovely shops

Castello Aragonese

WALK 12
Procida

The low-key sights of the bay's smallest, least touristic island can be seen in a morning, followed by a lazy lunch in a picturesque marina, and an afternoon spent lounging on one of the unspoilt beaches.

DISTANCE: 6km (3.75 miles)
TIME: A leisurely day
START: Marina Grande
END: Lido
POINTS TO NOTE: Procida is a 40-min hydrofoil ride from Naples (leaving from Beverello) and 10 mins from Ischia. The slower ferry from Naples' Calata Porto di Massa takes an hour. Procida is easily explored on foot, though there is also a good bus service between the Porto and Chiaiolello (www.procida.it).

At just 4 sq km (2.5 sq miles), **Procida** is the smallest of the islands. Fishing and farming are still funadmental to life here, and the volcanic soil is ideal for the cultivation of vineyards and citrus groves.

Marina Grande

Ferries and hydrofoils dock at **Marina Grande ❶**, a colourful jumble of boats and sun-baked houses – traditionally painted in different colours so that fishermen could recognise them from afar. The hill is dominated by the grim Castello d'Avalos, a prison until 1988. Turn left and meander along the harbour until you reach the church of **Santa Maria della Pietà** (1760) ❷. Stop for a coffee at the **Bar dal Cavaliere** opposite, see ❶, before taking Via Vittorio Emanuele uphill. Bear left at the yellow church to reach **Piazza dei Martiri** and the church of Santa Maria delle Grazie (1679).

It's a steep 500m climb from here to the crumbling **Abbazia San Michele Arcangelo ❸** (www.abbazia sanmicheleprocida.it), which has a coffered ceiling decorated with gold and a painting of the Archangel Michael by Luca Giordano (1699). There's also a museum and a set of catacombs.

The whitewashed domes of the abbey church rise above the **Terra Murata**, the ruins of a once-impregnable citadel. On your way back down to the Piazza dei Martiri, stop at the terrace of the abandoned Castello and admire the view.

Corricella

The fishing village of **Corricella ❹**, a warren of pretty pastel-painted houses, can be reached via the sloping road by

The town's colourful houses

hugging the coast, until you reach Via Solchiaro. Turn left then right into Via Simone Schiano, which leads to **Marina Chiaiolella** ❻, once the crater of a volcano and now a scene of yachts and fish restaurants; stop for lunch at **Crescenzo**, see ❷.

On the western side of the marina is the popular **Lido** ❼ beach. Buses L1 or L2 run from Chiaiolella back to the port.

the church. Take the steps to the left of the pink house for the harbour.

Another set of steps at the far end of Corricella takes you back up to the main road. Turn left into **Via Scotti**, whose high-walled gardens offer tantalising glimpses of citrus trees. Continue along Corso Vittorio Emanuele, turning left off **Piazza Olmo** on to the quieter Via Pizzaco, which commands glorious views across the bay. A little way along on your left, a flight of steps leads down to the lovely **Chiaia** ❺ beach, ideal for children, and **La Conchiglia** restaurant (see page 105).

Chiaiolella

Continue along Via Pizzaco, veering right into **Via de Gasperi**, and continue

Food and Drink

❶ Bar dal Cavaliere

Via Roma 42; tel: 081-810 1074; €
This *pasticceria* – founded back in 1960 – is a good place for a sweet treat – try the lemon or chocolate *lingua di bue*, a 'tongue' of flaky pastry. In summer it hosts regular party nights.

❷ Crescenzo

Via Marina Chiaiolella 33; www.hotelcrescenzo.it; €€
This harbourfront restaurant serves simply prepared fresh fish, right off the boat.

DIRECTORY

Our edit of the best hotels, restaurants and evening entertainment to suit all tastes and budgets, plus an A–Z of all the essential information you need to know, a quick language guide, and some great book and film recommendations to give you a flavour of the Naples.

Accommodation

Naples' fanciest hotels are concentrated on the seafront (Lungomare) around Castel dell'Ovo and in Chiaia, but for atmosphere you might prefer one of the newer boutique hotels set in historic *palazzi* in the centro storico. Budget hotels cluster around the station, but this is not Naples' nicest corner; it's worth spending more to stay in the centre. Sorrento is a good base for exploring the islands and the Amalfi Coast, and Naples is only a 40-minute boat ride or one-hour train ride away from there. Accommodation in the bay area is generally pricey, especially on Capri and in the main towns of the Amalfi Coast, although B&Bs and an increasing number of self-catering options listed on www.airbnb.com make a stay here viable for visitors on more limited budgets. Hotels get booked up well in advance, so reserve as early as possible; most hotels along the coast close between November and Easter.

Naples

Caravaggio
Piazza Sisto Riario Sforza 157;
www.caravaggiohotel.it; €€
This small 4-star hotel with just 11 simple but comfortable guest rooms is set within a historic seventeenth-century building in a wonderfully convenient location behind the Duomo.

Price categories

Price categories (for a double room in high season including breakfast):
€ = under €100
€€ = €100-200
€€€ = €200-300
€€€€ = €300-400
€€€€€ = €400 and over

Decumani
Via San Giovanni Maggiore Pignatelli 15;
www.decumani.com; €€
This hotel is set in the one-time residence of Cardinal Riario Sforza: an elegant high-ceilinged *palazzo* with a sumptuous breakfast salon that has to be seen to be believed. The rooms are spacious and tasteful, and the location in the heart of the *centro storico* is certainly hard to beat.

Excelsior
Via Partenope 48;
www.eurostarsexcelsior.com; €€€€
The grande dame of Naples' hotels, right on the waterfront, the *Excelsior* offers old-school glamour in spades. The rooms are spacious and wonderfully opulent; the bathrooms clad in marble. Head to the gorgeous top-floor terrace for breakfast or for a sunset cocktail in the summer months and get lost in the mesmerising, sweeping views of the bay.

The terrace at Grand Hotel Parker's

Grand Hotel Parker's
Corso Vittorio Emanuele 135;
www.grandhotelparkers.it; €€€€
Founded in 1870, this grand hotel is
away from the waterfront in fashionable
Chiaia. The rooftop George's Restaurant
and Bar offers candlelit dining at night,
and heart-stopping views of Vesuvius
and Capri by day. 82 rooms and suites.

Hotel Chiaja
Via Chiaia, 216 (1st floor); www.hotelchiaia.it; €€
Located close to Piazza Plebiscito, this
endearingly old-fashioned, vintage-
style hotel has ornately comfortable
rooms quirkily decorated with antique
furniture and is popular with musicians
and artists performing at the nearby
Teatro San Carlo. Staff are very helpful.

Exe Majestic
Largo Vasto a Chiaia 68;
www.eurostartshotels.it; €€€
Set between the centro storico
and Piazza Plebiscito, this is a very
practical, convenient place to stay,
offering comfort and convenience at
a reasonable price but without much
romance. It has a good buffet breakfast,
plus a fitness centre. 112 bedrooms.

Micalò
Riviera di Chiaia 88; www.micaloartrooms.it; €€€
Perfectly at home in chic Chiaia,
this boutique hotel has a distinctly
designer feel. Most of the rooms are
on two levels, with stylish bathrooms
up above. The acres of natural

The Excelsior's grand facade

materials and modern neutrals are
enhanced by an array of modern art
by young Neapolitan artists on the
walls. Excellent breakfasts, too.

Palazzo Decumani
Via del Grande Archivio 8;
www.palazzodecumani.com; €€
The sweeping spiral staircase at this
boutique hotel sets the tone for the
neo-Baroque decor throughout.
The rooms are very comfortable,
with luxuries such as plush chaises
longues and marble bathrooms
with Etro toiletries. The welcome
cocktail is a nice touch, too.

The lobby at Grand Hotel Parker's

A suite at Grand Hotel Parker's

Piazza Bellini
Via Santa Maria di Costantinopoli 101; www.hotelpiazzabellini.com; €€

Set over five floors of a historic palazzo, this hotel has been totally revamped and now boasts a fun, modern interior. The white walls, and the bright, contemporary rooms really make the hotel stand out among Naples' play-it-safe options. Staff are endlessly helpful and the location is a one of the best in the city – a stone's throw from leafy Piazza Bellini. They also have a lot of family rooms and several apartments.

Santa Lucia
Via Partenope 46, 80121; www.santalucia.it; €€€

One of a row of grand seafront hotels, in a prime position opposite the Castel dell'Ovo, which manages to be refined without being stuffy. Rooms are spacious, several have great views, and some have hot tubs.

Tribù
Via dei Tribunali 339; www.tribunapoli.com; €

In the heart of the *centro storico*, this small, stylish B&B is run by arty couple Gaetano and Alessandra, who are full of suggestions on how to plan your stay. Rooms are thoughtfully furnished, with interesting art and design touches, and breakfast is taken on the sunny terrace in fine weather. They also have an apartment in Amalfi.

Grand Hotel Vesuvio
Via Partenope 45; www.vesuvio.it; €€€€

With a prime position on this five-star strip, the Gran Hotel Vesuvio stands out for its charmingly old-fashioned feel and direct views of the Castel dell'Ovo. The rooms are as luxurious as you'd expect, and breakfast is a sumptuous banquet overlooking the waters of the bay. The great Neapolitan tenor Caruso was a frequent guest.

Camping in Naples

A list of campsites in Naples and surrounding areas can be found at www.camping.it/en/campania/napoli. Most sites get very crowded in summer, so book in advance.

Sorrento

La Badia
Via Nastro Verde 8; www.hotellabadia.it; €€

A small, pleasant hotel in a lovely restored abbey surrounded by citrus groves, on the clifftops above Sorrento town. Pool, restaurant and absolutely fabulous views. It's a steep walk but there are regular buses.

Casa Astarita
Corso Italia 67; www.casastarita.com; €€

Right on Sorrento's lively main drag, this superior and stylish B&B has individually furnished rooms, each decorated with a different colour scheme. You can use the library in the shared sitting room, and the free juices and water are a nice touch. Breakfast – with homemade cakes and jams – is a highlight.

Fantastic views over the harbour at Vesuvi

Towers Hotel Stabiae
SS 145 Sorrentina, km12, Castellammare di Stabia; www.towershotelsorrento.com; €€

An old cement works imaginatively converted into a stylish resort hotel with modern interiors, a fine pool and spa near Vico Equense on the Sorrento coast. Getting here is a little problematic if you don't have your own transport, but the food alone is worth it – being some of the best in the bay area. The prices for a standard double are at the lower end of this price category. They also have self-catering apartments and a wooden house right on the beach.

Grand Hotel Excelsior Vittoria
Piazza Tasso 34; https://excelsiorvittoria.com; €€€€

The most refined of Sorrento's grand clifftop hotels, the magnificent Grand Hotel Excelsior is separated from the riff-raff on busy Piazza Tasso by its beautiful, flower-filled gardens. There are elegant salons, terraces with stunning views of the bay, a breakfast room with a wonderful frescoed ceiling and a lovely pool surrounded by greenery. The hotel was once home to the great Caruso (with his suite available for special bookings). It's worth paying extra for a room with a sea view.

La Tonnarella
Via del Capo 31; www.latonnarella.it; €€€

A quiet clifftop hideaway, yet only a 10-minute walk into town. A few rooms have pine-shaded terracotta balconies and panoramic bay views. Small private pebble beach (with bar) is reached by a lift. Excellent restaurant and lunch can be served on the beach.

Ulisse Deluxe Hostel
Via del Mare 22; www.ulissedeluxe.com; €€

Thanks to the 'hostel' tag, Ulisse is off many tourists' radar, but banish all thoughts of dingy dormitories: a hostel in name only, this place has spacious private rooms with all mod cons, a swimming pool in the basement and a perfect location, midway between the town centre and the beach. Fifty rooms, including doubles, triples and quadruples. Male and female dormitories.

Amalfi

Floridiana
Via Brancia 1; tel: 089-873 6373; www.hotelfloridiana.it; €€

In a tranquil courtyard off Amalfi's heaving main street, this hotel has won awards for its customer service. The rooms are simple, bright and cheerful.

Anantara Grand Hotel Convento di Amalfi
Via Annunziatella 46; www.anantara.com; €€€€

A former monastery on the Amalfi cliffs, with delightful gardens and an Arab-Norman cloister to add to its panoramic views. The renovation has been carried out with style, creating a deluxe contemporary haven with

The Vesuvi Presidential Suite

marble bathrooms, with some features intact from the original monastery.

Hotel Luna Convento
Via Pantaleone Comite 33; www.lunahotel.it; €€€€

Ibsen penned much of The Doll's House in this marvellously romantic converted thirteenth-century monastery. In summer, breakfast is served in the Byzantine cloister, and rooms and the pool area (the pool is adjacent to the sea and is filled with sea water) enjoy wonderful views.

Marina Riviera
Via P. Comite 19; www.marinariviera.it; €€€€

This four-star hotel, set on a cliff overlooking the sea, has built up a loyal clientele thanks to its excellent service and attention to detail. Some of the rooms have been given a glamorous revamp, while others boast a more old-fashioned, breezy seaside décor. The beach is just a couple of minutes' walk away, but with the pool, the terrace on the sea and solarium, you might just be tempted to stay put. The hotel's gourmet restaurant, Terrazza 17, is highly regarded. There is also a spacious luxury self-catering apartment close by.

Sant'Alfonso
Via Sant'Alfonso 6, Furore; www.agriturismosantalfonso.it; €€

A stay in this excellent *agriturismo*, well off the tourist trail but only 8km (5 miles) from Amalfi, is a wonderfully peaceful experience. Set high up in the mountains with stunning views, this is a serene retreat with eight comfortable, cosily decorated rooms, welcoming hosts and heart-stopping views. There's a good on-site restaurant too; the food is accompanied by wine produced from the farm's vineyards. Resident goats and geese complete the bucolic scene.

Santa Caterina
Strada Amalfitana 9; www.hotelsantacaterina.it; €€€€

This is another of the coast's venerable hotels, carved into multiple levels of a cliff. Old-world and comfortably elegant, the hotel has a saltwater pool, lush terraced gardens, glorious views, a small private beach and respected restaurant – all further enhanced by a warm, highly accommodating, friendly staff. An easy walk from the bustling town centre.

Positano
Buca di Bacco
Via Rampa Teglia 4; www.bucadibacco.it; €€€€

With an excellent beachside location, acres of majolica tiles and antique furnishings, the Buca di Bacco has long been one of Positano's most desirable hotels so advance booking is essential. The rooms are traditionally furnished, though pale shades and French windows leading to sea-view balconies (in most rooms) give them a breezy feel. The hotel doesn't have claim to a section of beach, though a solarium is available for sun worshippers.

Excelsior Vittoria suite

Casa Albertina
Via della Tavolozza 3; www.casalbertina.it; €€€
This pretty family-owned guesthouse is not for the weak of knee: there are three hundred steps down to the beach, but it has exceptional views. Some rooms with balconies and Jacuzzis. Compulsory half-board in high season.

Hotel Rivage
Via Capo 11; tel: 081-878 1873; www.hotelrivage.com; €€
A great and reasonably priced hotel on the western edge of town. Most rooms have small terraces facing the water, and there's a pleasant restaurant with panoramic views.

Palazzo Murat
Via dei Mulini 23; www.palazzomurat.it; €€€
With an impressive historic pedigree – this was the home of Napoleon's brother-in-law Joachim Murat, who was also King of Naples – this beautiful hotel has been run by the same family for generations. Heirlooms and cool tiled floors set the tone; request a room in the older, more charming main part of the hotel. The lovely central courtyard, nestled among palm trees, trailing bougainvillea and other Mediterranean blooms, makes a lovely spot for breakfast, and for candlelit dinners.

Palazzo Talamo
Via Pasitea 117; tel: 089-875 562; www.palazzotalamo.it; €€€€

Fresh, bright rooms are painted in restful pastel hues that take their cue from the traditional majolica floor tiles. All have sea views and private terraces; those on floor minus-2 are the best. Family-run, the service is excellent, and there are several very good restaurants along this stretch, too.

Pensione Maria Luisa
Via Fornillo 42; www.pensionemarialuisa.com; €€
This reasonably-priced hotel has a friendly, welcoming feel. It's tucked away in a warren of whitewashed alleys in the Fornillo district – so walking back from the beach involves a slog up steep flights of steps. All of the rooms are pleasant and spotless, but it's definitely worth paying a little extra for one of the rooms with a huge sea-view terrace.

Poseidon
Via Pasitea 148; www.hotelposeidonpositano.it; €€€€
This hillside hotel is one of Positano's most pleasant and popular. Removed from the day-tripping buzz yet accessible to everything, it has a pool, beauty centre, gym and good restaurant. All rooms have terraces and lovely views.

Le Sirenuse
Via C. Colombo 30; www.sirenuse.it; €€€€
This beautiful luxury hotel is set in an aristocratic eighteenth-century building in town above the beach.

Excelsior Vittoria bay view

The pool at Santa Caterina

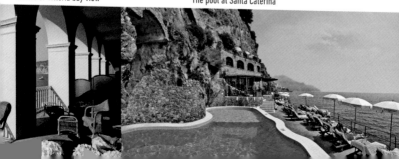

There are museum-quality family heirlooms throughout, wonderful open views of the sea and town, a stylish spa, an outdoor pool, a refined restaurant and its

Ravello

Palazzo Avino
Via San Giovanni del Toro 28;
www.palazzosasso.com; €€€€
Formerly known as the Palazzo Sasso, this twelfth-century aristocratic home has a gorgeous clifftop setting. One of the most fashionable and chic hotels around. Rooms are expensive, but they all have breathtaking sea views and are worth the premium. The food at gourmet restaurant Rossellinis is magnificent.

Parsifal
Via Gioacchino D'Anna 5;
www.hotelparsifal.com; €€€
Occupying a former monastery dating back to the thirteenth century, this charming small hotel, dotted with antiques, has a pleasantly old-fashioned feel, and the romantic terrace courtyard, with superb views of the sea below, is a plus. There's a restaurant; half-board is available on request.

Villa Cimbrone
Via Santa Chiara 26;
www.villacimbrone.com; €€€€
This stunning twelfth-century villa, renowned for its historic gardens, has hosted an array of famous names over the centuries, from Virginia Woolf to Bill Clinton. A 10-minute walk from Ravello's main piazza, with beautiful views at every turn, the hotel offers old-fashioned elegance rather than glamour, with traditionally styled rooms, gardens swathed in luxuriant blooms and a swimming pool with unrivalled sea views.

Capri

Capri Palace Hotel and Spa
Via Capodimonte 14, Anacapri;
www.jumeirah.com; €€€€
Impeccable service and supremely tastefully luxurious rooms – a handful with their own swimming pools – are features of this ultra-opulent five-star clifftop retreat. Capri's choice for the rich and famous, or a serious splurge. The hotel has several restaurants, including L'Olivo, which has two Michelin stars, and Il Riccio, a super-exclusive beach club.

JK Capri
Via Prov. Marina Grande 225;
www.jkcapri.com; €€€€
When Capri's narrow streets are crammed with day-trippers, retreat to this five-star bolthole, whose breezy, vaguely nautical decor is enlivened with quirky antiques and perfumed with the scent of freshly cut blooms. With four-posters in the rooms, balconies suspended over the sea and spectacular views, waking up here is a treat. And you'll have almost as

A luxurious suite at Le Sirenuse

much fun hanging out on the huge wrap-around terrace, lounging by the infinity pool or being pampered in the spa. Good restaurant too.

La Tosca
Via Dalmazio Birago 5; www.latoscahotel.com; €€

This small family-run one-star place a five-minute walk from the Piazzetta is a real find in Capri – early booking is a must. Among the spotless white rooms, no. 47 is the best, with its own sunny terrace offering lovely views over San Giacomo and the hillside. All rooms have air-conditioning and Wi-fi – a bonus in this price bracket. The management is very helpful, too.

Villa Sarah
Via Tiberio 3/A; www.villasarahcapri.com; €€

A relaxing hotel that's good value by Capri standards, in a tranquil setting, a 10-minute walk from the Piazzetta. The twenty rooms have balconies facing onto well-tended grounds, and breakfast is served on a pleasant garden terrace. There's a lovely pool, which is open from May to mid-October.

Ischia
Albergo della Regina Isabella
Piazza Santa Restituta 1, Lacco Ameno; www.reginaisabella.com; €€€€

One of the island's most upscale choices, the Regina Isabella is glamorous, but far from snooty: perfectly coiffed *signore* are happy

to be seen in their dressing gowns at breakfast, and the staff are endlessly helpful and welcoming. Some of the rooms have been given a modern makeover, but most are classic and old-fashioned. The spa is highly regarded, but is more for targeted therapies than indulgent pampering; the restaurant is excellent. Check the website for bargain low-season deals.

Il Moresco
Via E. Gianturco 16, Ischia Porto;; www.ilmoresco.it; €€

In the centre of Ischia Porto and just steps from its own private beach, this hotel is an excellent base for exploring Ischia. The decor is quite traditional in feel, and a certain old-world charm pervades: you can have aperitifs in the piano bar before moving through to the restaurant, where the dapper waiters are a paragon of old-fashioned service. The on-site spa has three pools and a raft of treatments. Half-board is usual in high season – and the restaurant is excellent.

Procida
La Casa Sul Mare
Via Salita Castello 13; www.lacasasulmare.it; €€

Procida's top choice is this enchanting hotel, set in a lovely eighteenth-century *palazzo*. Rooms are bright and simply furnished in aquatic shades, with balconies overlooking the sea and the picture-perfect fishing village of Corricella below. There is a lot of return custom, so book well in advance.

The historic Hotel Excelsior Vittoria.

Restaurants

In Naples the best fish restaurants and more up-market establishments with bay views are found in the Borgo Marinaro area, and in Santa Lucia, Mergellina and further west in Posillipo. For family-run trattorias, authentic pizzerias and cheaper food in general, head for the *centro storico*, where the exuberant atmosphere makes any meal memorable – even if it's just a slice of takeaway pizza.

In the more touristic coastal resorts, as a general rule, restaurants in the main piazza or on the waterfront will be more expensive; for a more authentic experience, head off the tourist trail.

Eating out is central to Italian culture, and a slap-up dinner on Saturday or lunch on Sunday is a time-honoured ritual; in view of this, booking ahead is always a good idea, particularly in high season.

Restaurants generally open for business at around 12.30pm, but Neapolitans don't tend to eat until around an hour later; in the evening, restaurants open at around 7.30pm to cater to tourists, but the locals are generally still quaffing *aperitivi* at that hour, heading from bar to restaurant at about 9pm. Many restaurants in Naples are closed on Sunday.

Price categories

Two-course meal for one with a glass of house wine:
€€€€ = over €80
€€€ = €50-80
€€ = €25-50
€ = under €25

Naples

Al Faretto
Via Marechiaro 127, Posillipo; www.alfaretto.it; €€
You need to make a little effort to get here as this is out on the north end of the bay in Posillipo. However, with fabulous fresh seafood, classic Neapolitan specialities and magnificent views thrown in, it's worth the effort.

Amici Miei
Via Monte di Dio 77–8, Chiaia; www.ristoranteamicimiei.com; €€
Small, dark and intimate restaurant, long loved for its meat specialities and classic pastas. This being Naples, fresh seafood is given its fair share of attentive preparation: no one leaves disappointed, especially after sampling the homemade fruit tarts.

Antica Latteria
Vico Alabardieri 30; www.anticalatteria.it; €
Just off lively Piazza dei Martiri, this bustling, cheerful place takes its name

Dining with a view

from its origins as a dairy, and the simple, *osteria*-style decor and wood-beamed ceiling retain the old-fashioned feel. The honestly priced dishes are excellent value in this part of town.

La Chiacchierata
Piazzetta Matilde Serao 37; tel: 081-411 465; €
A tiny family-run trattoria, La Chiacchierata – 'the chatterbox' – is one of the best places to have a meal in the historic centre. Neapolitan specialities are naturally the staples, such as tender polpette (octopus) and hearty bean-based soups. Reservations are recommended.

Ciro a Santa Brigida
Via Santa Brigida 71; www.ciroasantabrigida.it; €€
Since opening in 1932, this has been an institution for regulars including Toscanini and Pirandello. Off the store-lined Via Toledo, the two-storey restaurant is always busy. Offers pizzas or a lengthy menu of classic Neapolitan dishes served by friendly house-proud waiters.

Da Michele
Via Cesare Sersale 1-7; www.damichele.net; €
In business for over one hundred and forty years and still going strong, this venerable pizzeria only serves two types of pizza – the classic *margherita* and the *marinara* (with a topping of tomato, garlic, oregano and olive oil) – but they are king-size and near-perfect. The decor is minimalist in the extreme – simple marble-topped

The two choices at Da Michele

tables and a vast pizza oven take up most of the space – but it has a legion of fans. Be prepared to queue.

Fantasia Gelati
Piazza Vanvitelli 22; www.fantasiagelato.it; €
There are always hordes of people devouring ice creams on the pavement outside this excellent *gelateria* in Vomero's lively main piazza, and a permanent queue inside – which at least gives you time to choose which of the fifty-plus flavours to go for.

Friggitoria Vomero
Via Cimarosa 44; tel: 081-578 3130; €

Antipasti selection

Pasta at Mimì alla Ferrovia

This Vomero institution is a great place for lunch on the run, offering fried specialities such as slices of battered aubergine, incredibly good value at just €0.20. There are sweet treats too – try the *graffe*, sugar-coated Neapolitan doughnuts. Its takeaway only – enjoy your picnic in the tranquil Villa Floridiana, a short stroll away.

Il Gobbetto
Vico Sergente Maggiore 8;
www.osteria-il-gobbetto3.webnode.it; €
Tucked away in the Quartieri Spagnoli district, this is an utterly authentic Italian trattoria, with traditional dishes

(though no pizza) at very low prices. The pasta dishes are excellent, thanks to the freshness of the ingredients, and the sea bream baked in salt is a standout *secondo*. Booking essential.

Gran Caffè La Caffettiera
Piazza dei Martiri 26;
www.grancaffelacaffettiera.com; €
This local favourite, in Chiaia's main square, is busy throughout the day: Gucci-clad *signorine* perch on the high bar stools to sip a morning *macchiato*, office suits pop in for a panino or a sugar-dusted pastry, and a dressed-up evening crowd gossips over *aperitivi* on the decked terrace.

La Locanda del Grifo
Via F. Del Giudice 14;
www.lalocandadelgrifo.com; €
This pizzeria-restaurant enjoys an atmospheric location, with outdoor tables on a pretty *centro storico* square just off hectic Via dei Tribunali. The huge pizzas are the draw here, but the menu also offers a handful of mainly fish-based *secondi*. Look out for the griffin that gives the restaurant its name, perched on the campanile opposite.

Mimì alla Ferrovia
Via Alfonso d'Aragona 21;
www.mimiallaferrovia.it; €€
In business for seventy years and still a bastion of old-fashioned service, this traditional trattoria is an unlikely survivor in the culinary wasteland around

Inside Naples' Mimì alla Ferrovia

the central station – great if you have a train to catch. Downstairs is buzzy at lunch, while the more elegant first floor is more atmospheric at dinner.

Osteria Da Carmela
Via Conte di Ruvo 11–12; www.osteriadacarmela.it; €
A meal at this homely one-room *osteria*, with doily-covered tables and family paintings on the walls, feels somewhat like dinner at your elderly aunt's house. The menu is equally lacking in pretension, with a handful of simple *primi* and *secondi*. A bonus is the in-house art gallery, promoting works of emerging artists.

Palazzo Petrucci Pizzeria
Piazza San Domenico Maggiore 5–7; www.palazzopetrucci.it; €
Definitely one of the best pizzerias in town. Efficient service and reasonable prices make the Palazzo Petrucci a great pit stop, set in an amazing seventeenth-century palazzo.

La Scialuppa
Borgo Marinaro 4; www.lascialuppa.net; €€
Bag a table on the flower-filled terrace or soak up the atmosphere in the dining room, with huge windows overlooking the Borgo Marinaro. Fish is the speciality, but you can order a pizza and enjoy the same views for a fraction of the price.

Un SorRiso Integrale
Vico S. Pietro a Maiella 6; www.sorrisointegrale.com; €

The perfect antidote to pizza and pasta overload, this organic vegetarian restaurant-cum-health food store is in a small courtyard off Piazza Bellini. With fresh flowers on communal wooden tables and crates of fresh produce dotted around, it has an appealingly homespun feel, and the food's good, too: big salads, soups, cheese plates and home-made cakes. The piatto unico, with a selection of seven different dishes, is especially great value.

Taverna dell'Arte
Rampe S. Giovanni Maggiore 1A; www.tavernadellarte.it; €€
Hidden away on a side street near Via Mezzocannone, this is many people's idea of the perfect little Italian trattoria: terracotta-tiled floors, walls lined with wine bottles and simple white linen on the tables; four tables sit under a flower-strewn bower outside. Simple, well-executed dishes include meatballs with local greens and home-made soups (no pizza).

Campi Flegrei
Grottino a'Mmare
Via dell'Emporio 15, Pozzuoli; €€
A smart choice, with simple, elegant table settings on a decked terrace overlooking the water, this place has been serving up the freshest of the day's catch since 1912.

Pompeii
Il Principe
Piazza Bartolo Longo 8; tel: 081-850 5566; www.ilprincipe.com; €€

Cappuccino

Al fresco dinner in Naples

If you haven't packed a picnic for Pompeii and fancy a splurge, this prestigious restaurant is the place. The regional dishes are excellent, and most people opt for one of the set menus.

Sorrento and the Peninsula

Il Buco
Rampa Marina Piccola 2a, Sorrento; www.ilbucoristorante.it; €€€€

Don't be fooled by the name ('The Hole'): this is Sorrento's top restaurant. Eat in the ancient brick-arched dining room or outside on stepped terraces. The restaurant is tucked into the stone vaults of the Basilica di Sant'Antonino.

La Conca del Sogno
Via Amerigo Vespucci 25, Nerano; www.concadelsogno.it; €€€

Finding this tucked-away restaurant is not easy, but worth the effort. As you drive down towards Marine del Cantone, after Nerano follow signs to the Villaggio Syrenuse. Ask for permission to drive through this campsite, beyond which the road cuts through a ravine and opens out on to a tiny beach and the lovely Conca del Sogno – an excellent restaurant that also has six rooms. Call if you want their shuttle boat to pick you up from Marina del Cantone.

Da Franco
Corso Italia 265, Sorrento; €

This rowdy locals' pizzeria is at Corso Italia's non-touristic end. Take a seat at one of the communal wooden tables and watch your pizza being prepared by one of the expert *pizzaioli* in the open kitchen. The house special is topped with tomato, cheese, rocket and parmesan, but there are plenty of other options to tempt you, too.

Don Alfonso 1890
Corso Sant'Agata 11–13, nr Sorrento; www.donalfonso.com; €€€€

Pilgrims of gastronomy know the 7km (4.5-mile) drive from Sorrento to the hills 365m (1,200ft) above sea level is a price willingly paid for a meal at one of Italy's finest and most renowned restaurants, the proud holder of two Michelin stars. Superchef Alfonso Iaccarino uses produce from his farm to create the culinary masterpieces his family's long-established restaurant is renowned for. The award-winning wine cellar is one of the largest and best in Italy (and that's saying something). The dining room is suitably elegant – all Murano glass and hand-painted majolica – and the tasting menus are very tempting indeed. Book well in advance if you want to experience this place. There are rooms if you wish to stop overnight, and a cookery school.

La Fenice
Via degli Aranci 11, Sorrento; tel: 081-878 1652; www.ristorantelafenice.com; €€

This restaurant/pizzeria is attractively decorated and has a welcoming atmosphere. Seafood and antipasti

Freshly-prepared squid

are the specialities, on a menu that
has something for all budgets.

Sant'Antonino
Via Santa Maria delle Grazie 6, Sorrento;
www.ristorantesantonino.com; €€

Right in the centre of Sorrento but
tucked away in an elevated position
up a flight of steps, this restaurant is
a hit with locals and tourists alike for
its delicious food and jovial service.
There are no bay views, but dining
on a terrace full of citrus trees makes
up for it; look out for the hybrid that
grows both oranges and lemons.

Taverna del Capitano
Piazza delle Sirene 10–11,
Marina del Cantone; tel: 081-808 1028;
www.tavernadelcapitano.com; €€€€

Marina del Cantone is renowned for
its fish restaurants, and this is one
of the best. With a Michelin star
and a stellar reputation, it invites
high expectations, and the superb
fish dishes don't disappoint. The
dining room is lined with inlaid
wood, and the wine cellar, set in the
cherry-wood hull of a reproduction
Sorrentine ship, is fabulous.

Amalfi

Da Gemma
Via Fra Gerardo Sasso 11;
www.trattoriadagemma.com; €€€

This landmark trattoria, in business since
1872, is famous for its fish soup and its
surprisingly delicious aubergine-and-

Il Buco

chocolate dessert, but there are many
standout dishes. Whether you eat inside
in the spacious, airy dining room or
on the elegant roof terrace with views
of the Duomo, booking is essential.

Dolceria dell'Antico Portico
Salita Antonio Tirabasso, 2; tel: 089-871 143; €

This boutique *pasticceria* in the heart
of Amalfi is an essential stop for
foodies. The owner, Tiziano Mita, is
a whiz with pastry, taking the long-
established Neapolitan tradition to
new heights; his *sfogliatella* is given a
new twist in the shape of a *trullo* – the
typical Puglian conical-roofed house

Pistachio ice cream in town

The view from Rossellinis

– while the traditional *delizia* lemon-cream cake is paired with an olive-oil biscuit. Melt-in-the-mouth lemon and almond pastries are another speciality.

Pansa
Piazza Duomo 40, Amalfi; www.pasticceriapansa.it; €

This historic *pasticceria* is an elegant spot for a coffee and pastry, lined with vintage wood cabinets and age-spotted mirrors. For breakfast go for a sfogliatelle, and for an afternoon treat e sure to try one of Pansa's citrus specialities: *delizia al limone*, stuffed with lemon cream and flavoured

with *limoncello*, or chocolate-coated candied orange peel.

Ravello
Rossellinis
Palazzo Avino, Via San Giovanni del Toro 28; www.palazzoavino.com/en/ Dining/Rossellinis; €€€€

In the opulent surroundings of the Hotel Palazzo Avino, this restaurant has a splendid setting, its terrace perched high above the bobbing lights of the fishing boats below.

Villa Maria
Via Santa Chiara 2; www.villamaria.it; €€€

Relaxed yet refined, this is one of the prettiest settings for lunch with a bird's-eye panorama, or for dinner with a high romance quotient. Classical music drifts through the pergola-covered alfresco terrace and cosy indoor dining room of this century-old villa that also offers a dozen rooms. The chef knows his regional specialities, beginning with the homemade spaghetti-like scialatielli that are typical of Naples.

Positano and environs
Buca di Bacco
Via Rampa Teglia 8; www.bucadibacco.it; €€

One of the most enduring of the beachfront see-and-be-seen scenes. Its best main courses are the simply grilled fresh fish. Book early for the railing-side tables with a view of the action below. A pre-dinner drink at the first-floor open-sided bar is de rigueur.

Lunch in Amalfi

Chez Black

Via del Brigantino 19; www.chezblack.it; €€

A stylish, fashionable restaurant that is one of a cluster snuggled directly on the beach. It offers very good-quality food and value-for-money considering its prime location and long-time popularity. For an informal lunch or relaxed dinner, it's one of the better choices in town for great pizzas and pastas, with reliably fresh fish for more serious dining.

Da Vincenzo

Viale Pasitea 172–178; www.davincenzo.it; €€€

This family-run restaurant is not the cheapest in town, but worth the splurge for the outstanding cooking and local delicacies that you'll only find here: fish and seafood dominate, cooked with creative flair. Neapolitan music in the evening adds to the buzzy atmosphere.

Donna Rosa

Via Montepertuso 97–99, Montepertuso; www.donnarosapositano.it; €€€

Just above Positano, the quieter, more workaday village of Montepertuso harbours several very good restaurants, but Donna Rosa is the standout choice, and is packed with dressed-up locals every night. The expertly prepared seafood is the main draw, although the stunning views come a close second. Leave room for dessert – the hot chocolate soufflé is to die for. The restaurant will pick you up from Positano at a set time. Booking essential.

Capri

Aurora

Via Fuorlovado 18, Capri; www.auroracapri.com; €€€€

This is one of Capri's smartest restaurants, where you may find dishes such as fish carpaccio with vanilla salt and pine nuts, and linguine with lobster and asparagus, though (pricey) pizzas are on offer, too. The elegant terrace dotted with pots of fragrant blooms is right on Capri's main shopping strip, making it prime people-watching territory – book for dinner for a more tranquil experience.

Canzone del Mare

Via Marina Piccola 93; www.lacanzonedelmare.com; €€€€

In the former home of English singer Gracie Fields, this resort hotel embedded in the rocks was a jet-set destination in its heyday, and remains a little reminiscent of the 1960s. The location of the terrace restaurant remains as stunning as ever, beside a swimming pool surrounded by gardens with views of the Faraglioni, and the food is of good quality, if expensive. The names, meaning 'Song of the Sea', refers to the hauntingly beautiful singing of the sirens, who lured sailors to their death on the rocks.

Da Alberto

Via Roma 9–11; www.baralbertocapri.com; €

In business since 1946, Da Alberto is a good spot for a coffee and a wedge

Fresh clams

You won't go short of pasta in Naples

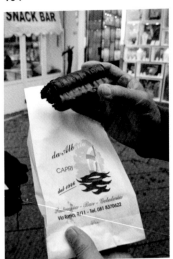

Pastry from Da Alberto

of *torta caprese* – Capri's deliciously moist almond-and-chocolate namesake. In August, the bar is famous for its *cornetto caldi* (hot-from-the-oven croissants), served all night long to bleary-eyed bar-hoppers.

Da Paolino
Via Palazzo a Mare 11, Marina Grande; www.paolinocapri.com; €€€€
You may find yourself fighting Hollywood A-listers for a table at one of Italy's most romantic restaurants, where the candlelit tables, piled high with mouth-watering antipasto, are set amidst the lemon groves. Save up for a splurge and book well ahead.

Seafood pizza

La Pigna
Via la Palazzo 30; www.caprigourmet.it; €€€€
With gorgeous views over the Gulf of Naples, this elegant restaurant is the perfect place for a romantic dinner, especially if you can get a table on the terrace. The food, which is served with flair, combines local and international influences.

Pulalli
Piazza Umberto 4; tel: 081-837 4108; €€
Wonderfully sited in the bell tower overlooking the Piazzetta, this elegant restaurant and wine bar is reasonably priced (for Capri). *Scialatielli verdi* (pasta with prawns and rocket) is the house speciality, and the walls are lined with over three hundred wines. Book to be sure of a table on the terrace.

Terrazza Brunella
Via Tragara 24; www.terrazzabrunella.com; €€€€
Near Punta Tragara, a 10–15 minute walk from the Piazzetta, is this atmospheric restaurant, with a spectacular clifftop perch offering breathtaking views – booking a table by the window is a must. The food is excellent: try the lobster linguine or the king prawns with cognac.

Ischia
Calise Caffè Concerto
Piazza degli Eroi, Ischia Porto; tel: 081-991 270; €

An Ischian institution, this vast place is a bar, *pasticceria* and pizzeria in one, and even a club in the summer months, with live music nightly. Its lushly planted gardens make a great place for an *aperitivo*, and if the chattering crowds get too much, there are plenty of little hidden corners to retreat to.

Da 'Peppina' di Renato
Via Montecorvo 42, Località Forio; www.trattoriadapeppina.it; €€
Furnished with old barrels, this enticing *trattoria* offers hearty local cuisine, such as *zuppa di fagioli* (pasta and bean soup with porcini mushrooms, sausage, escarole and lemon). Reservations are essential.

Neptunus
Via lo Russo 1, Forio d'Ischia; www.ristoranteneptunus.com; €€€
Perched on a cliff and enjoying spectacular views, this colourful restaurant has a vibrant atmosphere in the evenings, when there's live musical entertainment. Its fresh-off-the-boat fish, expertly prepared, attracts the great and the good and photographs of VIP visitors are proudly displayed.

Umberto a Mare
Via Soccorso 2, Forio; www.umbertoamare.it; daily noon–11pm, closed Nov–Mar; €€€
This upscale restaurant offers panoramic views and superb fish dishes. At lunch, you can feast on dishes such

Pulalli

as linguine with tuna, capers and olives. There's also an elegant café.

Procida
La Conchiglia
Chiaia beach; www.laconchigliaristorante.com; €€
Right on Chiaia beach, La Conchiglia is a wonderful place for a family lunch (this is one of the safer beaches for children) or a romantic dinner, with views to swoon over. Pasta with mussels and courgettes is a speciality *primo*, and the grilled fish is superb. No road access; take a taxi boat from Corricella or walk down the steps from Via Pizzaco.

Coniglio all'ischitana pasta

Freshly picked lemons

Essentials

Age restrictions

The age limit for consuming and purchasing alcohol in Italy is 18. Stricter penalties on establishments selling to those under 18 have been enacted. The minimum age for driving, provided you hold a full licence, is 18 but for renting a car in most cases a driver must be 21 or over.

Budgeting

Naples is relatively inexpensive, though prices soar in resorts along the Amalfi Coast and on Capri. The following is a general guide to give you an idea of how to budget.

Food and drink

A glass of house wine in Naples will cost around €5, on Capri €10; a beer is €3 in Naples, at least €6 in Capri. At an inexpensive trattoria, pasta and main courses go for around €10; in moderate places, €13--15; in expensive restaurants €25 and upwards.

Hotel prices

Hotel rates vary hugely, but a double room in a cheap hotel in Naples will cost under €100; a moderate hotel €100-200; in low season it can be possible to find deluxe rooms for as little as €150, though in high season the sky's the limit.

Transport costs

Public transport is cheap: a 90-minute ticket within Naples is €1.50, or a weekend day from Naples to Sorrento just €4.50 (valid for 180 minutes). Hydrofoils are pricier: around €16 one-way from Naples to Capri, though slower ferries and the Metrò del Mare summer services are a little cheaper.

Entrance charges

The major museums and archaeological sites charge from €5 to €20. Most state-run museums and sites offer free entrance to EU citizens under 18 or over 65, with a lesser discount to those aged between 18 and 25. Many state museums offer free entrance on the first Sunday of each month. Entrance to most churches is free.

Campania Artecard

If you are planning to see quite a few sights during your trip, the **Campania Artecard** (www.artecard.it) could be a worthwhile investment. Several varieties are available; one particularly useful option is the Napoli Card, which gives free access to the first three of the many key attractions in Naples, plus half-price entry on all remaining sights. It also includes the

Family fun on a moped

use of the public transport system (valid for three days). The three-day Tutta la Regione card includes even more sights, including Campi Flegrei and Pompeii. Buy the card online, at participating museums, at tourist offices or from the Artecard info-point in the central station.

Children

Feeding children in Naples and along the coast (and indeed in the rest of Italy) isn't usually a problem, since most kids like pasta and pizza. Most find the ice creams delicious, too. Neapolitans, like all Italians, are very fond of children (over-indulgent if anything), and big family meals are the norm in restaurants so you are unlikely to encounter any places that turn their noses up at younger customers.

Disposable nappies (diapers) and baby food and formula milk are as easy to buy in Italy as in most of Europe and the US. You often get a wider selection in pharmacies than in supermarkets.

Nappy-changing facilities are not widely available, although you will usually find them in more upmarket restaurants and, if you are driving, at motorway service-station toilets.

Bring your own pushchair and baby carrier, as you are unlikely to find them for hire. However, child seats are usually available as extra items when hiring a car.

Kicking a ball around on Piazza del Plebiscito

Child-friendly sights and attractions

In terms of places to take children, the Villa Comunale has plenty of space for kids to let off steam, as well as an aquarium, and the Parco di Capodimonte is a good place to kick a ball around.

Older children might enjoy a visit to Pompeii or Herculaneum – especially if it's preceded by a virtual-reality reconstruction – or the intriguing underground sights of Napoli Sotterranea and the catacombs, or the geological wonders of Vesuvius and the Solfatara.

A busy beach in Ischia

Naples' Palazzo Reale

The Città della Scienza (Via Coroglio 104; www.cittadellascienza.it; charge) is part of the redevelopment programme of the old Bagnoli steelworks. In March 2017 a brand new 3D Planetarium with 120 seats and CORPOREA, the first human body museum in Europe, will be opened to the public. The hi-tech hands-on science park is a fun day out for children and adults; take bus R7 from Naples' Piazza Vittoria.

Hiring a boat in Sorrento, the Amalfi Coast or the islands and pottering between beaches can be a fun way to spend a day.

And if all else fails, take the kids to **Edenlandia** (Viale Kennedy 76, Fuorigrotta; www.edenlandia.it), a traditional theme park just outside Naples. Take the Cumana train from Montesanto to get there.

Clothing

Light summer clothes are suitable from spring to autumn. The heat is sometimes alleviated by a sea breeze by day and evenings can be cool, even in summer, so keep a jacket to hand. Hats and sunglasses are recommended for sun protection.

Rainfall is rare in mid-summer, but when the deluge does come, it's often a surprise afternoon shower that rarely lasts very long. November to January is notoriously rainy, so bring a raincoat. In winter, you'll want to dress in layers.

Crime and safety

Despite its reputation as a hotbed of crime, Naples is no more dangerous than any other big European city, if you take the usual precautions. The main problem tourists experience is pickpocketing and bag-snatching, together with theft from parked cars.

Wear bags across the body if possible and be wary of nimble-fingered lads whizzing by on mopeds. Be especially vigilant on crowded buses and around Piazza Garibaldi, the Quartieri Spagnoli and La Sanità.

Report a theft *(furto)* as soon as possible; you will need to go to the police to make a statement *(denuncia)*. The police report will be required for any insurance claim and to replace stolen documents.

For information on the nearest police station, call Naples' Questura Centrale, near Piazza Municipio at Via Medina 75, tel: 081-794 1111, or ask for the *questura più vicino*.

Customs

Free exchange of non-duty-free goods for personal use is allowed between EU countries. The following are the guidance levels:
Tobacco: 800 cigarettes, or 400 cigarillos, or 200 cigars, or 1kg of tobacco.
Spirits: 10 litres above 22% strength or 20 litres below 22% strength.
Wine: 90 litres (only 60 litres can be sparkling).

A romantic moment in Naples

Beer: 110 litres.

People travelling from non-EU countries should refer to their home country's regulating organisation for a current complete list of import restrictions.

Disabled travellers

Central Naples is not an easy place for people with disabilities. However, things are improving, with ramps and lifts being installed in museums, stations and hotels. Capri's hotels in particular are good at meeting individual needs, and as there are no steps, it can be easier to get around, though the slopes are steep and buses are not wheelchair-accessible. An accessible route at Pompeii makes navigation of the site easier for those with reduced mobility.

Call 199 303 060 for assistance on trains, and 848 888 777 for help at the airport.

The website www.accessibleitaly. com is useful for pre-trip planning, and www.turismoaccessibile.it is another excellent resource, with detailed information on accessible museums, restaurants and hotels.

Electricity

Standard is 220 volts. Sockets are generally two round pins.

For UK visitors, adaptors can be bought before you leave home, or at airports and stations. Travellers from the US will need a transformer.

Embassies and consulates

If you lose your passport or need other help, contact your nearest national embassy or consulate.
Australia: Australian Consulate General www.italy.embassy.gov.au
Canada: Canadian Consulate www.canadian-consulate.com
New Zealand: Consulate General www.mfat.govt.nz
Republic of Ireland: Honorary Consulate, www.dfa.ie
UK: British Consulate General www.british-consulate.org
US: US Consulate General, https://it.usembassy.gov

Emergency numbers

National emergency number, including police and medical emergencies: tel: 113
Carabinieri: tel: 112
Ambulance: tel: 118
Fire: tel: 115

LGBTQ+ travellers

Attitudes towards LGBTQ+ relationships in Naples and the main resorts are reasonably tolerant, though smaller towns may be more conservative. The national organisation Arcigay www.arcigay napoli.org offers information and advice, and organises events for the local gay community. *Rough Guide to Top LGBTQ+ Friendly Places in Europe* is another useful source of information and advice.

Sunset on the Amalfi Coast

Enjoying the evening sunshine

Health

All EU countries have reciprocal arrangements for reclaiming the costs of medical services. UK residents and non-EU members should have private travel insurance that covers medical care, emergency repatriation costs and additional expenses such as accommodation and flights for anyone travelling with you.

A pharmacy (*farmacia*) is a good first stop for medical advice. The name of the duty or all-night pharmacy is posted on pharmacy doors.

Chemists

Chemists (*farmacie*) have a large green cross on the outside. The pharmacy at Napoli Centrale station is open 7am–10pm; *Il Mattino* newspaper carries details of late-night pharmacies. For more information, and listings, visit www.farmaciediturno.net.

Emergencies

If you need emergency treatment, call 118 for an ambulance or information on the nearest hospital with an emergency department (*pronto soccorso*).

Hospitals

Naples' most central hospitals with *pronto soccorso* (emergency) departments are in Vomero: Cardarelli at 9 Via Cardarelli; tel: 081-747 1111 and Santobono

(for children under 12) at 6 Via Mario Fiore; tel: 081-220 5734.

Hours and holidays

In general, shops open Mon–Sat 9am–1pm and 4–7pm or 8pm, although the bigger ones now stay open later, and even open on Sundays. Most restaurants close on Sundays. Many shops and restaurants close for at least two weeks in August. Banks generally open Mon–Fri 8.30am–1.30pm and 2.45–4pm. Some branches may also be open on Saturday mornings.

Opening times of churches and museums vary enormously and change twice a year, with a longer timetable for summer (Easter–Oct) and a shorter one for winter (Nov–Easter). Most churches open early in the morning but close at around noon or 12.30pm until 3pm or 4pm, closing again in the evening between 7pm and 8pm; some open in the morning only.

Many museums are closed on Monday and ticket offices close one hour before the official closing time. Archaeological sites close one hour before sunset; two hours in the case of Pompeii and Herculaneum.

Most businesses are closed on the following public holidays:
New Year's Day (1 January)
Epiphany (6 January)
Easter Monday (date varies)
Liberation Day (25 April)

Piazza Plebiscito in Naples

Labour Day (1 May)
Founding of the Republic (2 June)
Assumption of the Virgin Mary (15 August)
Feast of San Gennaro (Naples only, 19 September)
All Saints' Day (1 November)
Immaculate Conception (8 December)
Christmas Day (25 December)
St Stephen's Day (26 December)

Internet facilities

All major hotels, shopping malls, post offices and cafes in Naples offer Wi-fi.

Money

Currency

The unit of currency in Italy is the euro (€), which is divided into 100 cents. There are 5, 10, 20, 50, 100, 200 and 500 euro notes, coins worth €1 and €2, and 1, 2, 5, 10, 20 and 50 cent coins.

Credit and debit cards

ATMs are widespread and have instructions in the main European languages, though an increasing number of places accept contactless payments, so it is no longer necessary to carry wodges of cash around. Major credit and debit cards are accepted by most hotels, shops and restaurants, and the number of places remaining cash-only are steadily diminishing. Cash machines (ATMs), called Bancomat, can be found throughout central Naples and the main resorts, and are the easiest and generally the cheapest way of obtaining cash; in smaller towns ATMs are scarcer.

Changing money

You need your passport or identification card when changing money. Not all banks will provide cash against a credit card, and some may refuse to cash traveller's cheques in certain currencies. On the whole, exchange bureaux *(cambio)* outside of touristic areas offer better rates than banks.

Tipping

Most hotel prices are quoted as all-inclusive *(tutto compreso)*, meaning the service charge is included. Many restaurants impose a cover and bread charge *(coperto and pane)*, although officially it has been eliminated. Often, a 10–15 per cent service charge *(servizio)* is added to the bill; if not, it is usual to leave 10–15 per cent. Hotel porters, maids and doormen, bartenders, toilet attendants and service-station attendants expect a tip of €1–2. For taxi drivers, round the fare up to the nearest euro. If you have a tour guide, a tip is expected, but how much you give depends on the service you receive and the size of your party.

Posing in Pompeii

Post

Post offices normally open Mon–Fri 8.35am–1.35pm, Sat 8.35am–12.35. Only main post offices in major towns open in the afternoons, usually staying open until 19.05 (www.poste. it). Stamps *(francobolli)* can also be purchased from tobacconists.

Italian postboxes are usually red with two slots, *per la città* (for the city) and *tutte le altre destinazioni* (everywhere else).

Stamps *(francobolli)* can be bought at many tobacconists *(tabacchi)* – look for the sign with the white letter 'T' on a black background. For fast delivery (up to three days in Europe and five to the rest of the world), ask for *posta prioritaria* (priority post) stamps.

Smoking

Smoking is banned in all indoor public spaces in Italy, except in those establishments that have created a specially ventilated smoking area, though this is rare.

Telephones

Dialling codes and useful numbers
The prefix for Italy is +39.
The local code is 081.

When calling abroad from Italy, first dial 00 (the international access code), then the country code (44 for the UK; 353 for the Republic of Ireland; 1 for the US and Canada; 61 for Australia; 64 for New Zealand), the area code and then the subscriber number.

Mobile phones
Mobile phones. UK mobile (cell) phones can be used in Italy, but check roaming rates with your provider before you leave – some charge no roaming fees for the first couple of weeks, but this varies and may change. It may be worth buying an Italian SIM card, available from any mobile-phone shop and many newsagents, for longer stays. The new small independent operators often have the best pay as you go deals – newsagents are usually well informed.

Time zones

Italy follows Central European Time (GMT+1). From the last Sunday in March to the last Sunday in September, clocks are advanced one hour (GMT+2).

Toilets

Bars are obliged by law to let you use their toilets. This doesn't mean that they will do so with good grace; if you don't spend any money at the bar first they may throw you a look. In many cases bar toilets are locked and you will need to ask for the key *(chiave)* at the till; once inside you may find out that there is no soap or toilet paper.

Café on the Borgo Marinaro

Tourist information

ENIT is the Italian Government Tourist board (www.enit.it). The official tourist offices in Naples are at 7 Piazza del Gesù, 9 Via San Carlo, and at the airport. The tourist board's website (www.infoturismonapoli. it) is useful with listings of hotels, shops, places to eat, guided tours, transport and any upcoming events. Elsewhere in Campania, tourist offices often struggle to keep open – those that are, are listed on the Region of Campania's official site (www.agenziacampaniaturismo.it).
Campi Flegrei: 3 Via Campi Flegrei, Pozzuoli, tel: 081-526 2419.
Pompeii: Piazza Porta Marina Inferiore 11, tel: 081- 850 8451.
Sorrento: 35 Via L. De Maio, tel: 081-878 2104.
Positano: 4 Via del Saracino, tel: 089-875 067.
Amalfi: 27 Corso Repubbliche Marinare, tel: 089-871 107.
Ravello: 10 Piazza Duomo, tel: 089-857 096.
Capri: 1 Piazza Umberto I, Capri Town, tel: 081-837 0686.
Ischia: 116 Corso Vittorio Colonna, tel: 081 991 464.
Procida: Via Roma, tel: 081-810 1968.

Tourist information abroad
Italian Government Tourist Board: 1 Princes Street, London W1R 8AY; tel: 020-7408 1254.

Italian Government Tourist Board: 686 Park Ave, New York 10065; tel: 212-245 5618.

Tours and guides

City Sightseeing open-top buses run on two lines in Naples (www.napoli. city-sightseeing.it), all of which depart from Piazza Municipio.

Transport

Arrival by air
Naples' airport is at Capodichino, 7km (4 miles) from the city centre; www.aeroportodinapoli.it.

Allow at least 20 minutes for the taxi ride from the airport to the centre of Naples (fixed fare €18). To check official fixed price fares to destinations within and beyond Naples see www.comune.napoli. it/flex/cm/pages/ServeBLOB. php/L/IT/IDPagina/20778.

The Alibus bus (www.naples-airport.info/bus) service runs regularly (every 20–30mins) to Piazza Garibaldi (15–20 mins) and on to Piazza Municipio (30–35 mins). You can purchase tickets on the bus or from teh desk inside the main terminal. Curreri buses (www.curreriviaggi.it) run every 75 minutes to Sorrento from outside the arrivals hall (1hr 15 mins); it's worth taking note that the same bus will also make stops at Pompeii at a passenger's request.

Market fish stall   Stunning view of the Amalfi Coast

The Alibus at the airport

Arrival by boat

Frequent hydrofoils from Sorrento, the Amalfi Coast and the islands dock and run services to and from Naples' port, Molo Beverello. Some services run from the islands and Pozzuoli to the smaller port of Mergellina, connected to the city by metro line 2. Larger, slower ferries from the islands arrive at Calata Porto di Massa, a 10-minute walk east of Molo Beverello. For schedules, check the daily paper *Il Mattino*, or ask at one of the tourist offices.

Arrival by road

From the UK, the usual route is through France, entering Italy at the Alps and taking the autostrada down to Naples.

Arrival by rail or bus

Most trains from other parts of Italy and Europe arrive at the main station, **Napoli Centrale** (www.napolicentrale.it) in Piazza Garibaldi, while high speed trains often also stop at the astonishing new Afragola station, designed by the late Zaha Hadid. Metro and suburban rail lines pass through the Stazione Centrale, and outside is a terminus for city and long-distance buses. From Piazza Garibaldi, take bus 1 to the port area, metro line 2 to Montesanto or bus R2 for the *centro storico*, or metro line 2 to Amedeo or Mergellina for Chiaia.

Public transport

The transport network within the bay area is very efficient and all the major sites and resorts are well served by buses, trains and boats. Pompeii, Herculaneum and Vesuvius are easily reached by train on the Circumvesuviana line from Sorrento or Naples. Towns in the Campi Flegrei area are served by the Naples Cumana and Circumflegrei regional metro lines (formerly the SEPSA lines). Transport connections between the islands and coastal resorts are efficient and reasonably priced. Ask at the tourist office for the free transport map.

Neapolitan guards

Tickets. UnicoCampania tickets (www.unicocampania.it) are available in various different forms covering the whole region, and are sold online and in *tabacchi* shops. Within Naples, you will need a UnicoNapoli ticket, available as a 90-minute ticket, all-day pass, or a weekly pass. Alternatively, the Artecard passes allow free travel on public transport within the covered area (the entire of Campania). There are also cheaper ANM and EAV tickets, starting at just €1.00, that cover only one journey, using only one line, with no interchanges, that are supplied by two independent companies.

On board buses, stamp your ticket in the machine; on metros, it needs to be stamped at the entrance gate before you get on.

Buses. Progress through the traffic-choked streets is often painfully slow. The main intersection is Piazza Municipio (bus stop outside the Castel Nuovo) and Via San Carlo (bus stop outside Galleria Umberto I). The most useful lines are: R1 (for the Archaeological Museum and Piazza Dante), R2 (to the train station), 140 (Riviera di Chiaia and Mergellina), R4 (Capodimonte).

SITA buses (www.sitasudtrasporti.it) have the Sorrento peninsula and Amalfi Coast covered. Buses from Sorrento to Positano and Amalfi depart in front of the main station (for Ravello you need to change at Amalfi). SEPSA buses serve the Naples suburbs and the Campi Flegrei. Two routes on Ischia circumnavigate the island; on Capri there are regular bus services between the major points of interest; buses on Procida link the port to the main villages.

Metros. The metro, currently being extended, can be very useful, especially Line 2, which stops at Piazza Garibaldi, Montesanto (for Via Toledo and connections to the Campi Flegrei), Piazza Amedeo (for Chiaia and the Vomero funicular), Mergellina and Pozzuoli. Line 1 runs between Piazza Dante, Museo (for the Archaeological Museum) and northeast Naples via Piazza Vanvitelli (Vomero); when complete, this line will be circular and link the city centre and the airport. Services operate 6am–11pm, with trains every 8–12 minutes.

Funiculars. Naples' funiculars serve the Vomero district. The Funicolare Centrale leaves from the bottom end of Via Toledo, the Funicolare di Chiaia from Piazza Amedeo and the Funicolare di Montesanto links Montesanto station to Via Morghen (nearest to the Vomero attractions). For more details, see www.anm.it.

Trains. Napoli Centrale can be a confusing place to catch a train to or from. The main train station (www.napolicentrale.it) is on the ground floor; downstairs are the metro

Arriving by train

and Circumvesuviana services (for Pompeii, Herculaneum and Sorrento; www.sitabus.it/circumvesuviana-orari-e-tariffe). To catch a Circumvesuviana train (roughly every 30 minutes), it's less of a headache to go to the more orderly terminus at Porta Nolana, just a few streets south.

Cumana trains (www.eavsrl.it) for the Campi Flegrei depart from Montesanto station (Metro line 2) in the centre of town.

Tickets for Trenitalia trains can be bought online picked up from one of the self-service machines in the station, where you can also buy your tickets directly. Buy UnicoCampania tickets for Circumvesuviana and Cumana services from the ticket office at the terminus of the line or from *tabacchi* shops. The stops along the line are divided into various fare zones. Tickets for all trains must be stamped before boarding at one of the yellow machines or they are not valid for travel.
Ferries. There are frequent ferry crossings between Naples, the islands and Sorrento. In summer there are ferry services that run to the Amalfi Coast towns, too. Hydrofoils *(aliscafi)* depart from Molo Beverello, near Castel Nuovo, the smaller port of Mergellina to the west and Pozzouli. The main operators are Caremar (www.caremar.it), Snav (www.snav.it), NLG (www.navlib.it), Alilauro (www.alilauro.it) and Gescab (www.

gescab.it). All hydrofoil timetables are listed on the Metro del Mare website (www.metrodelmare.it).

Ferries *(traghetti)* are slower, but you can sit on deck and take in the coastal scenery as you go. Caremar has the inter-island monopoly and Medmar (www.medmargroup.it) runs an Ischia service. All ferries leave from Calata Porta di Massa, a 10-minute walk from Molo Beverello. There are also services to Ischia and Procida from Pozzuoli.
Taxis. Official rates for taxis can be downloaded from the city council website (www.comune.napoli.it/flex/cm/pages/ServeBLOB.php/L/IT/IDPagina/20778) If the meter *(tassometro)* isn't switched on, point this out to the taxi driver, or agree a fixed price *(tariffa fissa)* before starting off. Water taxis also operate in the coastal resorts and island ports.

Driving
Unless you want to venture off the beaten track and explore the hinterland, driving is not a sensible option for getting around Naples and the Amalfi Coast: the traffic is horrendous (particularly along the Amalfi Coast in summer), parking is a problem, and if you're not used to driving in Italian cities, the general disregard for the rules of the road will do little for your stress levels.

If you're determined to drive, note that Naples' *centro storico*

The original Fiat 500

is off-limits to non-residential vehicles at certain times of the day (look for the ZTL – *zona a traffico limitato* – signs), and that you cannot take a car on to Capri.

Car and scooter rental. You can rent a car at the airport, though it's a good idea to book before you arrive. Rates are usually inclusive of insurance, but check to make sure you're completely covered. Most rental companies will supply a car with a full tank. E-bikes and e-scooters are less common than in other parts of Italy, so book in advance. CCT Bike Rental (www.cctbikerental,com) lists local rental agencies that have e-bikes and e-scooters.

The following companies have outlets at the airport:

Avis (www.avisautonoleggio.it)
Europcar (www.europcar.it)
Hertz (www.hertz.it)
Maggiore (www.maggiore.it)
Sixt (www.sixt.com)

Renting a scooter is to be avoided in Naples, but can be a fun way of getting around the islands; on Ischia, the largest island, you may be better off with a car. In the Amalfi Coast area, try Positano Rent A Scooter (www.positanoscooter.com).

Parking. In Naples supervised parking is a must. Parking lots *(parcheggio)* are marked with a blue 'P'. The most convenient is at the port, Molo Beverello (www.parcheggiobeverello.com; open 24 hours a day). You can also park along the blue lines in the city centre area (Mon–Sat); although hourly rates are pretty steep.

Outside Naples, make sure your hotel has parking facilities; Positano has several car parks in the upper town, but parking restrictions in Ravello and Amalfi mean you have to leave your car outside town.

Petrol. Petrol stations *(benzinaio)* are usually manned rather than self-service – just ask '*il pieno*', which means 'fill her up'. Most stations accept credit cards, but it's a good idea to carry cash in the off chance that they don't.

Visas and passports

EU and UK passport-holders do not need a visa to travel to Italy; a valid passport (or ID card is sufficient. Visitors from the United States, Canada, Australia and New Zealand do not require visas for stays of up to three months.

Nationals of most other countries, including South Africa, do need a visa to enter Italy. This must be obtained a few months in advance of travel from the Italian Consulate.

Ferry at Procida   A fully loaded scooter

Language

Italian is relatively easy to pick up, especially if you have any knowledge of French or Spanish (or a grounding in Latin). Most hotels have staff who speak some English, and unless you go well off-the-beaten-track, you should have little problem communicating in shops or restaurants. However, there are places off the tourist circuit where you will have the chance to practise your Italian, and local people will think more of you for making an effort. Here are a few basics to help you get started.

Useful phrases

General
Yes *Sì*
No *No*
Thank you *Grazie*
Many thanks *Mille grazie/Tante grazie*
You're welcome *Prego*
All right/That's fine *Va bene*
Please *Per favore/Per cortesia*
Excuse me (to get attention) *Scusi*
Excuse me (in a crowd) *Permesso*
Could you help me? (formal)
Potrebbe aiutarmi?
Certainly *Ma, certo/Certamente*
Can you show me…?
Può indicarmi…?
Can you help me, please?
Può aiutarmi, per cortesia?

I need… *Ho bisogno di…*
I'm lost *Mi sono perso*
I'm sorry *Mi dispiace*
I don't know *Non lo so*
I don't understand *Non capisco*
Do you speak English/French/ Spanish? *Parla inglese/francese/spagnolo?*
Could you speak more slowly? *Può parlare più lentamente, per favore?*
Could you repeat that please?
Può ripetere, per piacere?
How much does it cost? *quanto costa?*
this one/that one *questo/quello*
Have you got…? *Avete…?*

At a bar/restaurant
I'd like to book a table
Vorrei prenotare un tavolo
Have you got a table for…
Avete un tavolo per…
I have a reservation *Ho prenotato*
lunch/supper *il pranzo/la cena*
I'm a vegetarian *Sono vegetariano/a*
I'm vegan *Sono vegano/a*
May we have the menu?
Ci dia la carta?
What would you like?
Che cosa prende?
I'd like… *Vorrei…*
mineral water fizzy/still *acqua minerale gassata/naturale*
a bottle of *una bottiglia di*
a glass of *un bicchiere di*
red/white wine *vino rosso/bianco*
beer *una birra*

Newspaper kiosk

Numbers

One *uno*
Two *due*
Three *tre*
Four *quattro*
Five *cinque*
Six *sei*
Seven *sette*
Eight *otto*
Nine *nove*
Ten *dieci*
Twenty *venti*
Thirty *trenta*
Forty *quaranta*
Fifty *cinquanta*
One hundred *cento*
One thousand *mille*

Getting around

What time do you open/close? *A che ora si apre/chiude?*
Closed for the holidays *Chiuso per ferie*
Where can I buy tickets? *Dove posso fare i biglietti?*
What time does the train leave? *A che ora parte il treno?*
Can you tell me where to get off? *Mi può dire dove devo scendere?*
Where is the nearest bank/hotel? *Dov'è la banca/l'albergo più vicino?*
On the right *a destra*
On the left *a sinistra*
Go straight on *Va sempre diritto*

Online

Does it have wireless internet? *C'è Wi-Fi*

What is the WiFi password? *Qual è la password Wi-Fi?*
Is the WiFi free? *Il WiFi è gratis?*
How do I turn the computer on/off? *Come si accende/spegne il computer?*
Can I…? *Posso…?*
access the internet *collegarmi (a Internet)*
check e-mail *controllare le e-mail*
print *stampare*
plug in/charge my laptop/iPhone/iPad? *collegare/ricaricare il mio portatile/iPhone/iPad?*
How do I…? *Come…?*
connect/disconnect *si collega/scollega*
log on/log off *login/logout*
What's your e-mail? *Qual è la sua e-mail?*
My e-mail is… *La mia e-mail è…*

Social media

Are you on Facebook/Twitter? *È su Facebook/Instagrar? (polite form) Sei su Facebook/Instagram ? (informal form)*
What's your user name? *Qual è il suo nome utente? (polite form) Qual è il tuo nome utente? (informal form)*
I'll add you as a friend. *La aggiungerò come amico. (polite form) Ti aggiungerò come amico. (informal form)*
I'll put the pictures on Facebook/Twitter. *Metterò le foto su Facebook/Twitter.*
I'll tag you in the pictures. *La taggherò nelle foto.*

Expressions in grafitti

Sgraffito

Books and Film

The unique charms of Naples and the Amalfi Coast have long inspired creatives. Naples' unabashed exuberance has lured a legion of writers, from Charles Dickens to Graham Greene, while the stunning natural setting make the region effortlessly film-worthy.

Old books

Books

The Ancient Shore, Shirley Hazzard. An eloquent love letter to Naples, by an American writer who lived in the city for decades. This book collects Hazzard's best writings, interspersing them with evocative photographs.

Capri and No Longer Capri, Raffaele La Capria. A nostalgic portrait of Capri from the time of Homer to the present day.

Cosi Fan Tutti, Michael Dibdin. In the fifth book of the popular Aurelio Zen detective series, Zen is putting Naples and its shady criminal underworld to rights. A sparkling holiday read.

Falling Palace, Dan Hofstadter. A powerful homage to the author's beloved Naples, and the local woman who captivated him. The colourful character studies of the author's Neapolitan friends are priceless.

Greene on Capri, Shirley Hazzard. For more than forty years, Graham Greene spent part of the year at his villa in Anacapri. Hazzard's memoir stems from her long friendship with the writer, offering an intriguing glimpse into his life and a bygone Capri.

My Brilliant Friend, Elena Ferrante. First of the famously pseudonymous Ferrante's quartet of novels about childhood friends, Elena and Lila, who grow up together in the outskirts of Napoli during the 1950s. As they grow older, their paths repeatedly cross. It is also a tale of a changing neighbourhood, city and country.

Naples '44, Norman Lewis. Lewis' memoir of his time as an intelligence officer in a war-torn Naples is a fascinating and often harrowing account of a city on the verge of collapse, and its people surviving on their wits. A must-read.

Pompeii, Robert Harris. A pacey thriller that brings that fateful day

A scene from the film *Gomorrah*

in 79 AD to life. Harris' masterful recreation of everyday life in ancient Italy makes an enjoyably explosive read.

In the Shadow of Vesuvius, Jordan Lancaster. Exploring three thousand years of Naples' history, and touching on art, literature, cuisine, music, film and popular culture, this book provides a useful and readable overview.

The Story of San Michele, Axel Munthe. The heartwarming story of Munthe, a Swedish doctor, and his discovery and restoration of a crumbling villa on Capri, the Villa San Michele – now one of the island's biggest draws.

The Volcano Lover, Susan Sontag. Set in eighteenth-century Naples, Sontag's celebrated historical romance portrays the famous love triangle between Sir William Hamilton, his wife, Emma, and her lover, Lord Nelson.

Film

Gomorrah (2008). Unsettling film adaptation of Roberto Saviano's novel of the same title, providing a chilling exposé of Naples' most infamous criminal organisation, the Camorra. The film was produced by Matteo Garrone, who used the city's run-down suburbs as a set and cast untrained locals as actors.

Gomorrah TV series (2014-16). Based on Roberto Saviano's novel, this critically acclaimed production provides a fascinating insight into mafia hierarchy, from the perspective of both the foot soldier, and the *capo di tutti capi* (boss of all bosses).

L'Oro di Napoli (1954). Naples-born comic genius Totò joins Sophia Loren in this collection of six vignettes set in Naples.

Marriage Italian Style (1964). Vittorio de Sica's romantic comedy, featuring both Sophia Loren and Marcello Mastroianni, which launched the pair into international stardom.

Passione (2010). This documentary by actor-turned-director John Turturro is a passionate tribute to Naples' songs and singers.

Il Postino (1994). Chilean poet Pablo Neruda is exiled to a small island in Italy and strikes up a friendship with the local postman. A heartwarming tale, partly filmed on a sun-drenched Procida.

Sciuscià (1947). A classic of Neorealist cinema by Vittorio de Sica, this moving film deals with the scugnizzi, Neapolitan street children, at the end of World War II.

It Started in Naples (1960). Fluffy romantic comedy starring Sophia Loren and Clark Gable, who fall in love on Capri.

The Talented Mr Ripley (1999). The much-loved dramatization of Patricia Highsmith's psychological thriller makes good use of Ischia and Procida's old-world charm.

Voyage to Italy (1954). Roberto Rossellini cast his wife Ingrid Bergman in this poignant tale of a marriage falling apart against the backdrop of Pompeii, Capri and Naples.

A scene from *Passione*

About This Book

CREDITS

The Rough Guide Pocket Walks & Tours series helps you discover the world's most exciting destinations through expert-curated itineraries: a range of walks and tours designed to suit all budgets, interests and trip lengths. These walks, driving tours and site excursions cover the destination's most classic attractions as well as a range of lesser-known sights, while food and drink stops for refreshments en route are highlighted in boxes. If you're not sure which walk to pick, our Best Walks & Tours for... feature suggests which ones work best for particular interests. The Introduction provides a destination overview, while the Directory supports the walks and tours with all the essential information you need, as well as our pick of where to stay while you are there and select restaurant listings, to complement the more low-key options given in the itineraries.

About the authors

Rough Guide Pocket Walks & Tours Naples and the Amalfi Coast was updated by Ros Belford. Her work builds on original content by Natasha Foges and Cathy Muscat. Ros Belford co-wrote the first edition of the *Rough Guide to Italy*, and has since spent most of her life exploring, living in and writing about the most amazing peninsula on the planet. Her travel memoir, *Children of the Volcano* (2024), about bringing her two young daughters up on a remote island off the coast of Sicily, is published by September Publishing.

Help us update

We've gone to a lot of effort to ensure that this edition of the **Pocket Rough Guide Naples and the Amalfi Coast Walks & Tours** is accurate and up-to-date. However, things change – places get "discovered", opening hours are notoriously fickle, restaurants and rooms raise prices or lower standards. If you feel we've got it wrong or left something out, we'd like to know, and if you can remember the address, the price, the hours, the phone number, so much the better.

Please send your comments with the subject line "**Pocket Rough Guide Naples and the Amalfi Coast Walks & Tours Update**" to mail@uk.roughguides.com. We'll acknowledge all contributions and send a copy of the next edition (or any other Rough Guide if you prefer) for the very best emails.

Credits

Pocket Rough Guide Naples and the Amalfi Coast Walks & Tours

Editor: Kate Drynan

Author: Ros Belford

Picture Editor: Tom Smyth

Cartography: Katie Bennett

Layout: Grzegorz Madejak

Head of DTP and Pre-Press: Rebeka Davies

Head of Publishing: Sarah Clark

Photo credits: Greg Gladman/Apa Publications 4BR, 6TL, 6MC, 6ML, 6BC, 7T, 7MR, 10L, 10/11, 11, 14, 15L, 14/15, 16, 17, 18, 18/19, 19L, 20, 20/21, 21L, 24/25, 30, 31, 32, 32/33, 33R, 34, 34/35, 35R, 37, 38, 39, 40, 41R, 40/41, 42, 42/43, 43R, 44, 44/45, 45R, 48/49, 51, 52, 53, 54, 54/55, 55R, 56, 57, 58, 58/59, 59R, 62, 63R, 62/63, 64, 64/65, 65R, 66, 71, 72, 72/73, 73R, 74, 75R, 77R, 78, 78/79, 79R, 82, 83R, 98/99, 99R, 102/103, 103R, 106, 107R, 106/107, 108, 109R, 110, 111, 112, 112/113, 113L, 114, 115, 116, 116/117, 117R, 119R, 118/119, 120T; Il Buco 101T; iStock 60, 61; Leonardo 88, 88/89, 89R, 90, 91, 92, 92/93, 93R, 94, 102T; Mimì alla Ferrovia 98T, 98; Moviestore/REX/Shutterstock 120B; Public domain 26, 48; Shutterstock 1, 4BL, 4MR, 4T, 7M, 7M, 8/9, 12/13, 22, 23, 25R, 26, 26/27, 27T, 27R, 28/29, 36, 46, 47, 49R, 50, 67, 68/69, 70, 74/75, 76, 76/77, 80, 81, 82/83, 84/85, 86/87, 89T, 95, 96, 97T, 97, 100, 101, 102, 104, 104T, 104/105, 105T, 107T, 108/109, 114T, 118; Skydancers/REX/Shutterstock 121

Cover credits: Amalfi **Shutterstock**

Printed in Czech Republic

This book was produced using **Typefi** automated publishing software.

Distribution

UK, Ireland and Europe
Apa Publications (UK) Ltd
sales@roughguides.com

United States and Canada
Ingram Publisher Services
ips@ingramcontent.com

Australia and New Zealand
Booktopia
retailer@booktopia.com.au

Worldwide
Apa Publications (UK) Ltd
sales@roughguides.com

Special Sales, Content Licensing and CoPublishing

Rough Guides can be purchased in bulk quantities at discounted prices. We can create special editions, personalised jackets and corporate imprints tailored to your needs.
sales@roughguides.com
http://roughguides.com

Index

MAP LEGEND

- ● Start of tour
- → Tour & route direction
- ❶ Recommended sight
- ◐ Recommended restaurant/café
- Ⓜ Metro station
- ★ Place of interest
- ⓘ Tourist information
- 𝟏 Statue/monument
- ✉ Main post office
- 🚌 Main bus station
- 🏛 Villa
- •⋯•🚠 Cable car
- ∴ Ancient site
- 🏰 🏚 Castle / ruin
- 🪨 Cave
- Park
- Important building
- Hotel
- Transport hub
- Shop / market
- Pedestrian area
- Urban area

NOTES